Meisje

I Met God in Hell

---•◦❧◦❧◦❧◦•---

A Young Girl's Journey to Forgiveness

Charlotte Van Steenbergen

ISBN 978-1-64416-266-8 (paperback)
ISBN 978-1-64416-267-5 (digital)

Christian Faith Publishing, Inc.
832 Park Avenue
Meadville, PA 16335
www.christianfaithpublishing.com

Printed in the United States of America

An Open Letter to My Readers

Dear reader,

Please know this is not a coincidence that you are reading this book. If you accidentally picked it up or it was a gift from a loved one, you will soon realize that a symphony, a tapestry, or a painting is being orchestrated, woven, and painted by God's hand with you as a participant, alongside Meisje as she shares how she was introduced to God in Hell by those who called on Him on a daily basis and by those who cursed Him daily. Hell was the nickname for Banyu Biru, Ambarawa. A concentration camp where she was imprisoned for three-and-a-half years as a young child.

Thank you in advance, dear reader, for being brave and willing to come alongside Meisje as she shares with you how God fashions lives together. Be assured that God knows who, what, and where you are. After all, you are created in His image and a much beloved child. So come and journey with Meisje as she navigates through the life that God designed, orchestrated, and purposed for her as well as for you.

Meisje (pronounced "May-sha") started having nightmares when she was an adult, recalling bits and pieces of her time in the concentration camp that began bubbling up to her consciousness—things she thought had been filed away so deep within as to never having to relive again. Apparently, that was not God's plan, for He awoke these memories from deep within to come to life, to be remembered, to be faced, to be processed, and shared.

He did this for the first time when she was on a trip to Israel and the surrounding countries. In fact, it was in Egypt where one day she saw a group of poor children begging alongside the road. One of the children squatted down in the dirt to relieve herself. As she watched the little girl, a flood of memories pierced her mind, heart, and soul.

3

Meisje recognized herself doing the same exact thing a very long time ago in the concentration camp. For her, it was on makeshift toilets, mere holes in the ground covered by bamboo planks. Careful, careful, scared stiff of falling in, avoiding contact with the overflowing feces and urine, remembering even the horrible stench, gagging and holding her breath!

Experiencing years of many more memories through nightmares and not recalling everything in the scary dreams, Meisje sought counseling through her church. Working with a therapist and God's loving mercy who let her recall only bits and pieces that she could handle, Meisje was able to face her demons by releasing fear and FORGIVING her captors, her tormentors. This was a process which took years and years of thoughtful and prayerful doing. She rarely has nightmares now and testifies that God has HEALED her.

Meisje truly can see God's hand of guidance and leading, as well as His protection throughout her life. Especially so, the healings and provisions during her captivity along with her rescue and liberation from the Japanese at the end of World War II. Thank God, He has restored her to wholeness—physically, mentally, as well as built her character and refined her soul, which continues to be an ongoing process.

Dear one, perhaps now a little biography on Meisje would be helpful, plus a background of geography and history as to where, when, and how her story began.

Meisje is a concentration camp survivor under the Japanese occupation in the Dutch East Indies during WWII. She is of Eurasian descent, part Dutch and part Chinese, raised with a Judeo-Christian upbringing with Dutch as her primary language. Both her parents' fathers (Meisje's grandfathers) were Dutchmen who married Chinese women when they left the Netherlands to live on the islands in the Dutch East Indies, which is now called Indonesia. Indonesia has a larger Muslim population than any other country in the world.

Meisje and her family were liberated in 1945 by the American and Allied forces, but unfortunately free for only ten days. They were then hauled back in to imprisonment, this time by the Indonesians who were fighting for their independence from the

Dutch, who had colonized the islands and held government control for hundreds of years.

Caught up in a horrible civil war known as the *Bersiap*, Meisje and her family fled the country in 1949; first by plane to another Indonesian island, and then by boat to Holland after a miraculous reunion with her father who had been declared dead by the Red Cross. The family lived in Holland for seven years and then immigrated to America in 1957. The family received permission to immigrate during a small window of opportunity for displaced refugees to come to the United States via a sponsorship under the Pastore Walter Act. They arrived by boat to New York, and then journeyed by train to California where she still lives today.

Meisje's story begins with an explosion—the attack on America. An airplane slams into the Twin Towers in New York, followed by a second plane, and then a third hits the Pentagon and a fourth crashes into a field in Pennsylvania. It was precisely when 9/11 occurred, as Meisje watched the news in horror and saw the images unfold on television; that her life took a dramatic turn and she started reliving the nightmares, putting things she remembered in writing in the form of poetry. One particular poem, which she titled "America's Gift," conceived and birthed from 9/11, became the basis for her speaking platform on gratitude. Especially focusing on veterans when sharing her story and poem, Meisje thanks the vets for having liberated her from the Japanese concentration camp—this prison in Banyu Biru in Ambarawa on the island of Java, in the Dutch East Indies during WWII, which was nicknamed Hell by those who lived through it.

This was Meisje's first introduction to God. In a horrific prison named Hell, she first learned of God by those who called and prayed to Him on a daily basis and by those who cursed Him daily.

Thank you, dear reader, for coming alongside on this journey!

Warmly,
Meisje

Chapter 1

You might wonder who Meisje is, well it's me! It's my nickname that my mother gave me. It means "little girl" in Dutch. I have found that writing, reporting, and seeing things through Meisje's eyes is not as painful nor as disturbing for me compared to if I were to write in the first person and relive the traumatic events again. So let's begin Meisje's story and come along for the journey.

Where were you when 9/11 happened? I'm sure, dear one, you remember vividly where you were and what you did on that day and the days following. I imagine it must have made an impression on you as well and perhaps impacted you as it did me.

Here in poetry form is my recollection of that horrific day.

9/11

Startled by the ringing of our phone early in the morning
I answered, to hear my daughter's anxious voice informing me
to turn on the television for an airplane had hit the twin towers
in New York! And indeed, it was as I watched in horror the images
unfolding on the screen … seeing, hearing, looking, as disbelief
and sickness in the pit of my stomach settled in.

I stayed glued to the television most of the day, numbed
to the core of my being, crying, shaking, and unable to
function. Seeing the chaos and shock on people's faces as
they ran for safety, as grayish smoke, soot, debris from
the first tower came down, soon to be followed by the
second tower as well.

Complete horror and flashbacks to my childhood came to mind, bringing back the fears and utter shock of attacks in the Pacific during WWII and incarceration in Ambarawa concentration camp.

Never in my entire life would I have imagined these feelings of so long ago, could surface in an instant and the trauma felt then, be so acute as I was feeling it right now. Experiencing the horror, helplessness, shock, and disbelief all over again!

As the days and weeks went by and numbness somewhat dissipated, the country came together as one big family. And the mourning process started for the three thousand losses we sustained, supporting our president and congress as war was declared on the terrorists who had inflicted this upon my beloved America.

A great deep love and concern flooded my being for those wanting to enlist to help and fight our enemy, to bring to justice those who had harmed us and for all the past veterans. Day and night, my love and gratitude deepened for our soldiers, past and present, to such an extent, that seeds for a poem were birthed, germinated, and came into being which I've titled, "America's Gift."

Chapter 2

As mentioned before, my journey started with an "explosion" on 9/11, and boy did it ever! Wounds that had been healed, so I thought, started bleeding profusely and painful memories came barreling up, shooting up, through to my consciousness. So many, so painful, I had to push them down, way down, only to trigger a series of nightmares.

Thank God for the support and understanding of a loving husband, God's mercy and grace as well as that of family and friends. They were so helpful, especially during those trying days, weeks, months, and years after the attack as nightmares began to surface again with recollected bit and pieces of fragmented memories. All so jumbled up because every time I woke up, only the memories of what I (my mind) could handle, would stay. Thank God for that! I learned early on that it was a good thing to have these nightmares as a form of release and healing, especially because God mercifully let me remember only what I could handle. Thus began my writing the bits and pieces of what surfaced and the "birthing" of poems. Truly a God thing! Maybe, dear one, females reading this have a better understanding or I should say have an easier understanding to why my reference to "birthing" is used for my poems—equating it going through birth pangs, pains, labor, and delivery.

In looking back, it pains and saddens me that my parents never received any counseling nor sought help for that matter, for what they endured while incarcerated—my father as a POW in Japan, and my mom, of course, in the same concentration camp as I was in. They just coped, sucked it up and learned to live with the horrific and traumatic experiences. They suffered and dealt with it as best they could, at times unknowingly causing and inflicting harm to themselves or others with their outbursts, their suppressed anger, erratic behavior, depression, and mood swings. Luckily today, for those who have gone through war and show a display of these same symptoms, we now know there is a name for it–post-traumatic stress disorder (PTSD).

I'm so glad I sought counseling early on as mentioned before. As a matter of fact, I did so not long after the first nightmares and episodes of memories appeared, triggered by seeing a little girl in Egypt squatting down relieving herself.

I have learned and come to realize that it's very hard and difficult for young children to process atrocities. Cruelty and brutality, punishment, torture, starvation, being ripped from home and familiar surroundings, separation from a parent, being denied the simple luxuries and comfort of a bed, clean clothes, a bath, food, regular meals, and school for a lengthy period of time and for whatever reason.

I remember vividly when we were taken, brutally ripped from our home by Japanese soldiers with bayoneted guns pointed at us, ordering and herding us into a truck. We had to step over a bloodied dead body with its stomach ripped opened with guts spilled onto the road. How can a scene like that ever be understood by a child? It's a hard thing to comprehend as an adult, let alone as a child who can't even begin to process it due to lack of knowledge and understanding. It took me years and years, lots of nightmares with the same dreams being repeated. Retaining what could be handled and filing away what could not, always seeing the bits and pieces of fragmented scenes through the eyes of Meisje, a little girl, until I could handle it and process it as an adult. Thank God! For truly it was by His grace and mercy that Meisje pulled through.

Dear one, here is the poem, birthed and titled "Taken" that describes that event in more detail.

TAKEN

Screams, footsteps, running, whispers …
  what is going on?
As she grabs her children and the baby
  to the safety of her room,
Pondering what to do after hearing
  They will come for her next!
She instructs her servants to grab valises,
  a duffle bag, suitcases, anything.
As chaos descended all around her
  she calmly packed things she and her
  two children could easily carry.

Soon heavy boots, banging, pounding
  and commands to "open up" came
Going to the door she instinctively shielded
  her children from the menacing scene!
Soldiers with drawn bayonets
  ordering her into a waiting truck.
As she tried to sidestep a bloodied body
  with its guts spilled onto the road
They forced her to step over it,
  handing the baby to strangers
  then helping her son and daughter.

Squeezed in the crowded truck
  she tried to make it a comfortable ride.
Settling her kids and few belongings
  on the floor bed of the truck.
Wondering where they're being taken to
  and why they were treated as prisoners.
Everything happened so fast, like a whirlwind,
  she needed to think clearly. Vowing,
To protect her children from harm,
  shield them from evil no matter what,
  praying they will stay together.

CHARLOTTE VAN STEENBERGEN

As more people were herded in,
belongings got tossed out.
Realizing this, she grabbed the pillow
which she brought along
To be used as a baby mattress,
dumping the duffle bag contents
In the pillow case, handing a doll
to her girl and toys wrapped in a
Kerchief, marbles, a sling shot
and pocketknife to her boy,
before tossing the duffle bag.
RELIEVED

Chapter 3

Dear Reader, how wonderful it is to be able to share that poem with you without the deep, traumatic, suppressed, and confused feelings of a child but that of a healed person, an adult in her later years; albeit with wounds healed and scars covered by scabs, which still can bleed at times.

So incredible the wits Mama had when making quick decisions on what to pack. Memories come to mind of the doll she handed Meisje in the truck, and the pocketknife and slingshot she handed her boy which became lifesaving tools in the camp to where we were transported.

Looking into my mind's eye as an adult now, back to Meisje in the truck, I see horror, shock, and disbelief etched on her face, akin to the faces of people I saw on television running away from the Twin Towers in the streets of New York. The same exact expressions! Of course, as it's true for the New York victims to show fear and feel shock, horror, and disbelief, the same is true as to what I see reflected on Meisje's face. Those were MY feelings as a child.

How I cowered, shaking uncontrollably with fear as I sat on the floor of the truck as more and more people were herded in and I got squished. I moved closer to my family and ended up sitting underneath my mother's legs as she sat on the truck bench and held the baby along with our belongings. Peeking from underneath my mama's legs to see what was going on, I see people getting slapped, pushed, stabbed—belongings thrown overboard to make room for more and more people.

Finally, it got so crowded that my mom who was very petite, ended up on the floor bed as well next to my brother. She yanked me out from underneath the bench to place my six-month-old baby sister there on the pillow she had brought along. Soon it got so crowded that my mom emptied the duffle bag to put all of its contents in the pillow case. She placed the baby on top of the uncovered pillow. Stuffing as many things into the pillow case as it would hold, even the baby's plate, bowl, little cup, spoon and fork, and handing Meisje (me) the doll, and my brother the slingshot, marbles, and pocketknife before throwing the duffel bag out of the moving truck. Relieved for herself and sad for others as she saw how some belongings, luggage, valises, rucksacks, and more were tossed out by our captors, the Japanese soldiers, without any regard to the owners as they tried to hang on to their precious cargo.

For hours and hours, we were in that truck, driving, picking up more people on the way. Crammed like sardines in a can, numb, fearful, wondering, hungry, and thirsty. Only nibbling on what was brought along. Seeing bloodied faces, hurt bodies, hearing cries, screams, witnessing struggles and fights, slapping, pushing—all these images etched in my memories—flashbacks, brought back to the surface on the day we were attacked right here on our own soil in America. I can clearly relate to both images and feelings; that of me riding away in the army truck on my way to be imprisoned in a concentration camp with all its horrors so long ago during WWII, to that of the images current of 9/11, the terror and horror, etched on those people's faces as they ran for their lives to safety.

Mama, so quick thinking, handed Meisje and brother what we thought were just toys but became lifesaving tools while in the camp. For me, it was just a doll and not even my favorite doll. Here is a poem about Dolly.

Dolly

Hunger ... hungry ... hungrier
   Empty ... emptier ... emptiest
      Skinny ... skinnier ... skinniest
DOLLY to the rescue ... Food
Sick ... sicker ... sickest
   Bad ... worse ... worst
      Weak ... weaker ... weakest
DOLLY to the rescue ... Medicine
Dark ... darker ... darkest
   Sad ... sadder ... saddest
      Less ... lesser ... least
DOLLY to the rescue ... Clothing
Hope ... hoping ... hopeless
   Dirty ... dirtier ... dirtiest
      Small ... smaller ... smallest
DOLLY to the rescue ... Soap

DOLLY ... not her prettiest or favorite
   Porcelain face, hands and feet
Body made of cotton, clothed in a
   Plain blue dress, with a white ruffled
      Pinafore, panties, socks and shoes.

DOLLY ... cut open, filling emptied
   Hastily stuffed with as many
Jewelry ... for emergency ... without
   Detection ... suspicion ... caught by
      Soldiers ... guards ... watchmen

DOLLY ... in her girl's innocent hands
   Oh, so dangerous ... representing
Food ... Medicine ... Clothing ... Soap
   Punishment ... Torture ... Sweatbox
      Necessary ... SURVIVAL ... Death

You know, dear one, it was a good thing I never knew how very important Dolly was for our survival during the whole duration of our incarceration. I truly marvel at the wits Mama had in selecting this doll over the others. Because it was my least favorite and not as pretty as other dolls, it made it less obvious for detection. Since she was ugly and my least favorite, I didn't show much interest, nor paid much attention to it other than Mama telling me to always hold onto Dolly and to never let her out of my sight.

Of course, years later Mama told me WHY she had selected that particular doll. She said it was because it had a fabric bodice and was easier to cut open so she could take out most of the cotton filling and stuff it with as many pieces of jewelry as it could hold. How clever of her—for indeed, the jewelry kept us alive. For every time the need for food, medicine, a bar of soap, clothing, or whatever need arose, she managed somehow to sell or barter a piece of jewelry. Albeit always at a very great risk of detection which usually led to harsh punishment, which she bore, many times over, for the sake of her children.

Chapter 4

After 9/11 and the birth of my poem "America's Gift," I began sharing the poem with my loved ones. Then my daughter who had shared my story with others, received invitations for me to share and recite the poem with our bible study group, soon followed by sharing it in front of the congregation in church. From there the poem took on a life of its own and my speaking engagements took off.

Invitations came from women's groups, churches, political clubs, and other organizations. The most rewarding and heartwarming were the ones booked with veteran organizations; with daughter next to me at the podium for moral support, introduction, and for a historical background on WWII in the Pacific theater.

Oftentimes when sharing my story with others, especially with vets, it turns into a thank-you and gratitude speech as my heart overflows with thanksgiving for the love and the way of life the American people have given me; first by liberating me from "hell," a nickname for the concentration camp I was in and later for welcoming me as a displaced refugee to making America my home.

Here is the poem, dear one, birthed out of the pains of 9/11, risen out of the ashes, soaring high, singing praises of hope, gratitude and thanksgiving!

America's Gift

Oh, America, when I first
  came and saw your beauty
  entering the harbor in New York.
Shivers of excitement and anticipation
  went through me
    Upon seeing a lady
      beckoning us
      holding high her torch
    The Statue of Liberty

Oh, a symbol so powerful
  speaking of, and representing
  the dreams, hopes and longings
  of its huddled masses
  who came before me.
Now offering all that and more
  once again to those who enter.

It is a cycle repeated over and over
as they come from all parts of the world.
Crossing the borders
    by land, sea, and air;
The poor, the broken,
    and the dreamers,
    all coming, wanting to know
      the way to freedom.

Oh, America, how can one not love you
    For is it not so, that it is
      because you loved first?

Now we can start healing our broken spirit
  and mend our body

So we can start
dreaming, working, and learning.
Yearning to integrate ourselves
to become one of mind, body, and soul.
A TRUE AMERICAN.

Oh, America, how I love you,
For opening wide your arms
to a wretch like me;
For reaching out with your infinite love
to rescue me, a stranger
a foreigner ... WHY?

Oh, America, I thank you,
For sending the masses
of sons and daughters to distant
land and shores far away.
To fight and risk laying down your life
so that I might taste your freedoms
enjoy your hospitality,
sanctuary and refuge.
And above all, to share in your wealth
and worship your GOD!

Oh, America, for that
I thank thee from the bottom
of my heart.
GOD BLESS YOU!

Coming to America from Holland in 1957 was a dream come true for Meisje (me). I lived in Holland for seven years with my parents and siblings after fleeing the war-torn country that I was born in. We went straight to a little village called Valthe in the province of Drenthe, close to the German border where a Dutch family took us in. My father knew their son, they had both served and fought in the Pacific theater during WWII for the Netherlands. Both never talked much about their service, experiences, and what they went through, but I imagine they became very close friends—precisely because of what they have gone through together. They had promised to help take care of each other if the need arose. I remember my father's friend saying, "If you ever need to flee, come to Holland, my home is your home!" That became a reality in 1949 when indeed we literally had to flee the Dutch East Indies during the civil war (Bersiap) when the Indonesians were fighting to gain their independence from Holland.

This was accomplished a few years later when the country became the Republic of Indonesia. We left behind everything when we came to Holland in 1949. We brought only the clothes on our backs and the basic necessities for starting over a new life with help of my father's friend and his family. I remember flying in a little plane and shots whizzing all around us as we flew away in the middle of the night from one island to another, where later we took a boat to Holland.

We were welcomed with open arms into their lives, home, and little town and received an overwhelming outpouring of love. Mind you, the citizens of Holland were also still recovering from war with Germany and their resources were depleted as well, yet they were gracious and loving enough to share what they had. To me it seemed like I had gone from hell to heaven—such a stark contrast!

What a difference to be able to live in a place and not have to hear any sirens or gun shots, see bullets flying about, war scenes, noise, chaos, and anything pertaining to war. Instead, we got to live in serenity, calm, and peaceful surroundings on a beautiful farmhouse with cherry orchards, with a loving Dutch family, and its village people. This is where we could regain back our health, sanity, and to recuperate. We stayed until we had enough strength, confidence, and resources to stand on our own two feet. What a precious gift these Dutchmen gave us.

The physical and mental respite in Holland gave Meisje the chance to somehow put aside the dark and horrific things from her mind. Filing away as it were, deep down into her consciousness, all those traumatic experiences endured during the war to concentrate on this new life in Holland. It was relatively easy to do. Because NOBODY talked about the trauma and hardship they went through nor was it shared.

It seemed everyone was busy, concentrating, and intending on making a new life. At least that is what my parents did as well as me! The first order of business was learning how the Dutch people lived their daily lives, so different it was from what we were used to. Even simple things like eating potatoes were their staple versus rice that was ours. Their mode of transportation was different—lots of bicycles! Also, the Dutch did everything themselves, they had no servants whereas we had servants helping us in our daily lives—a chauffeur, a cook, a nanny, and a gardener.

Back in my home country, some even had a seamstress and extra help for the cook or nanny, for example, each child would have his or her own nanny. This was a big change for us, and coping with the climate which was the biggest adjustment I believe. The language was no problem at all, nor the schools for we spoke Dutch and had attended Dutch schools on the islands. But Holland with its four seasons and harsh winters, is a country so opposite of the islands with its tropical climate. That took a lot of adjusting and it was very difficult, especially for Mama.

Looking back on those days in Holland, my soul wonders in amazement at God's hand—His guidance and His leading—how he placed me in Holland, the land of my forefathers, to replenish me, to learn, and grow. I was like a sponge soaking up all that Holland offered. I learned to trust, love, and respect its people, its beauty, its coziness, and the simple pleasures of life.

I came to love the four seasons, spring, summer, fall, and winter; teaching me that the rhythm, steadiness, and regular cycles in life could be attained, accomplished, and applied relatively in harmony.

There is a Dutch word, "gezellig" (pronounced he-SELL-ik), that has no accurate English translation but means cozy, friendly, from the heart, and is usually used in relation to time spent with loved ones. It is the perfect word I think of when I think of Holland. It's therefore with much fondness and appreciation I look back on our accomplishments.

The hard work that afforded us to live in a beautiful home in a city surrounded by forests, heather fields, and Stone Age hedges and which also had a zoo—the only one in Holland. This is where my father held three jobs and owned a car, so unheard of, since Holland is a land of bicycles. He was a high school teacher in Biology and Science, plus had a job tutoring students privately and was hired by an American company to teach their employees English and Dutch. Thank God we enjoyed a good life in this beautiful, small, cozy, Holland for seven years.

A country full of history and rich in its own unique culture, arts, and music! Holland with its windmills, tulips, their traditional costume, and wooden shoes; where they have dikes to keep the water at bay for the country lies below sea level, my dear sweet Holland, thank you for your LOVE! GOD BLESS!

Chapter 5

Coming to America was a Godsend for my mother for health reasons. Mama's worn-down body couldn't cope with the harsh Dutch weather after the war. While my father was researching countries that we could immigrate to, he heard about the Pastore Walter Act that was passed by congress in America for displaced refugees. This was an opportunity to enter the US legally with a sponsorship by individuals, churches, companies, or organizations who were willing to sponsor a person, a couple, or a family without burdening the taxpayers as we are seeing today with illegal immigration.

This was such an excellent concept, one that I wish America would implement again. For I know firsthand, the heart of the American people, which is their generosity, their willingness to help the downtrodden, the poor, the broken, and those who have lost their country.

I am one of them and a recipient as well. This heart of America should not ever be taken for granted nor should it be taken advantage of. I vividly remember how excited I was and all the detail, the preparation it took for immigration to America. I even remember the questions asked about my political affiliations and religious beliefs plus the medical exams I had to undergo. That is what they now call being vetted. Although the thought of starting all over again in a new country, this time with a new language which I did not speak was scary. It was all, well, worth it!

Meisje (I), soon learned that the people in charge of the program had found a church in beautiful California that was willing to sponsor and be responsible financially for the whole family for five years. Incredible! This was such wonderful news, especially for Mama who would benefit the most health-wise as California resembles most the tropical climate that would be conducive to her overall wellness.

Her poor body, mind, and spirit were broken down from our time in the concentration camp.

Here is a poem I wrote regarding my thoughts and feelings of immigrating to the United States of America, which I've titled "Refugees."

Refugees

Refugees coming to America
  by boat from Holland
    to settle in a new country.
Arriving in New York harbor
  The Statue of Liberty
    welcoming the new arrivals.
Processing the masses of people
  alphabetically in Grand Central Station
    to different parts of the country.
Then each person with passports,
  their luggage and bags, finally
    boarded the awaiting trains.
Assigned a roomy cabin compartment
  Meisje, her parents, and siblings
    settled in to travel across America.
Anticipating what lies ahead
Meisje with beating heart looks
  forward with hope to a bright future.
Amazed at the vastness, richness,
  Beauty, enormity of mountains,
    forests, lakes, prairies, and deserts.
Seeing, enjoying, curious
  wondering, learning, adapting,
    adjusting to all foreign and new.
Experiencing spectacular, colorful
  beautiful sunsets and sunrises in
    the heart of winter, RAYS OF HOPE.

Refugees—such a different meaning or portrayal today. When Meisje (I) came to America as a refugee, it was via a sponsorship; in my case, a church organization was willing to take us in, the whole family, and be responsible for us for five years so as not to be a burden to the American people—the tax payers. This was after having been thoroughly vetted.

As I mentioned before, immigrating here to America as legal immigrants versus illegal refugees makes a tremendous difference! It's a win-win situation for all parties concerned. No laws are broken as they come and enter by invitation. No financial burden on the tax payers, therefore, no cause for resentment, hate, demonstrations, or rioting because only those who can and are willing to help, shelter, and provide for these displaced refugees do so out of the goodness of their hearts.

Thousands of immigrants were helped this way, not only by churches of all denominations, but also by organizations, corporations, and individuals. Years ago when I was newly married, my husband and I reciprocated by sponsoring others as well, paying forward and doing the same thing—helping and be financially responsible to those we've sponsored for a duration of five years. Even up until now, hubby and I receive not only gratitude from the recipients, but feel BLESSED for having done that and for having experienced the saying "It is far better to GIVE than to RECEIVE!"

Looking way back to the day when she traveled from New York to California, Meisje vividly remembers the feeling of incredible excitement for this new adventure—traveling by train across America, seeing the vastness, the largeness, the scope, the differences, in and of every state. She was constantly amazed, in awe, and wonderment, enjoying the display of sceneries, landscapes, fields, prairies, lakes, rivers, mountains, and more. In anticipation of the journey that lay ahead for her and her family, Meisje felt so incredibly lucky to be in America—a DREAM come true.

Seven days of nonstop traveling finally came to an end when Meisje and her family arrived at their destination—Riverside, California. From the East Coast to the West Coast of America, the United States, the USA, such a BIG country ... California ...

Hollywood ... movie stars, cowboys and Indians, and cars, cars, cars. Lots of them in all sizes!

With their meager belongings in hand, Meisje and her family stepped off the train onto the Santa Fe railroad platform in the evening rain. They were instantly greeted by a welcoming party from the church with umbrellas and escorted toward waiting cars. After quick introductions were performed, they were whisked away in cars to their new residence—their very own home.

Dear one, I don't know if you can relate to the incredible feeling of pure joy and gratitude one feels upon arrival and seeing the wonder of a shelter being offered to a homeless family from a country they left behind by choice. The following is what I wrote, taken from my journal that I want to incorporate and share with you dear one, as well as a poem titled "Our House."

Riverside California

Finally, after crossing the oceans for more than a week from Rotterdam to New York and riding the rails for another week from coast to coast, we arrived at our destination Riverside, California. Night had fallen, rain was pouring, wind was blowing, palm trees swaying, welcoming committee waiting under umbrellas ready to greet the new immigrants. Soon we were standing on the platform at the Santa Fe railroad station with a few bags and luggage which comprised of the entirety of our belongings. Quickly, introductions and handshakes were exchanged by church members and sponsors before we were whisked away into waiting cars taking us to a three-bedroom house not too far from the train station. Then hurried good night and sleep well greetings were said as a key to the front door was pressed into our hands and we were left standing in front of the house.

Our House

In wonder, awe and disbelief, we stared at the house
lights streaming out the windows with a welcoming glow
beckoning us to enter its shelter which of course we did.
Immediately we felt its gentle embrace enveloping us
in the warm loving protectiveness of each and every room
from living to sleeping quarters, bathroom, and kitchen.
Investigating, touching, opening, discovering, learning,
seeing complete furnished rooms, kitchen cabinets
filled, a refrigerator stocked, a washer and wringer.
Wonder after wonder a television set discovered when
cabinet doors were opened, bicycles in the garage
for each child and even an automobile for father.
This lovely home, the church members and sponsors ...
embracing, enveloping, welcoming, these tired, poor
wretched, displaced refugees, really strangers ... why?
Amazement, wonderment, admiration, love, gratitude
thankfulness for America and its gracious people
filled our hearts, minds, and soul to overflowing.
"OUR CUP RUNNETH OVER"

Chapter 6

Meisje and her family settled in their new country, America. The beginning years were difficult especially learning a new language but oh-so necessary as well as finding jobs and going to school. We quickly learned we had to acclimate and immerse ourselves in not only the language but also the American culture. Fortunately, Meisje's Judeo-Christian upbringing was pretty similar to that of the American culture thus assimilating became easier. Within a short time of school, college, studies, helping at home, working part-time, and with the help from church and sponsors, Meisje fully embraced and accepted life in her new country.

Meisje's dream of living in the country of her liberators had come true and she is forever grateful. Coming to America as a seventeen-year-old teenager was such an amazing, wonderful WONDER! And now glancing back, she cannot but marvel at how beautifully God has orchestrated this journey in her beloved adopted country into this incredible symphony of Life!

The first ten years of her life were horrid, horrific, tormented experiences in her birth country, the Dutch East Indies. Things a child should never ever have to undergo, let alone experience, hence for her own preservation, she filed that part of her life away deep in her heart, mind, and soul.

Then came a time of seven years of emotional rest and physical restoration in the Netherlands. Holland—such a small, sweet, cozy, and picturesque country—where both of her grandfathers were from and where Meisje got to know that side of her heritage. A country so rich in history and antiquity compared to America.

What an incredible opportunity for Meisje when America opened up what she called a "window" of opportunity to enter by sponsorship. She will never forget the first impression of this big, modern, rich, and expansive new country. California, where she ended up living, with Hollywood, movie stars, and cowboys, teeming with shiny cars on its roads along beautiful homes, mansions, big tall buildings, high-risers in cities, towns, and communities. A state that is rich in everything commerce, population, natural resources, mountains, deserts, lakes, rivers, beaches, and even oil and gold in its soil. Perhaps one can see and appreciate all this only as an immigrant, and in my opinion, it should not be taken for granted as many who are born here do.

Even up until now, Meisje still vividly remembers all those early impressions and of being awed and overwhelmed by it as she soaked everything in like a sponge! Learning, earning, and yearning to become one with America and its people.

Here is a poem from Meisje's collection, dear reader, which she titled "Learning" that conveys what she was feeling.

Learning

Settling in ... adjusting, adapting to all things new.
  School, home, work, environment, American culture.
    Absorbing, learning, living, laughing, loving
      The many facets of life ... difficult, hard, intense.

Studying ... extra courses, cramming, graduating high
  School prepping for college, making friends, working
    Interning at hospital as aid and candy striper
      Volunteering ... earning credits toward units.

Receiving ... scholarship through friend's connection to
  Pepperdine University, our sponsor's gift to me.
    Visiting campus, buildings, classes, grounds, dorms
      Overwhelmed ... amazed by its beautiful surroundings.
        EXCITED ... SCARY ... GRATEFUL

Chapter 7

Meisje's first decade in America brought her so many first loves, including the "love" of her life, besides her love of country, its people, and everything America stood for. The love of her life came into her life accidentally, coincidentally, or was it by God's providence? Of course, you can decide for yourself, dear reader, but as for me I think it was God's hand that guided this young man from New Mexico to Riverside, California straight to Meisje's home.

It was not long after Meisje and her family's arrival in America, maybe a mere two or three months, when this young man came knocking on their door. The young man named Jimmy was invited in and never left, so to speak, as he ended up marrying Meisje several years later.

Here is a poem titled "Jimmy," rightly so, that describes that event.

Jimmy

A stranger came knocking on our door
  one beautiful spring afternoon.
He came all the way from Hobbs, New Mexico
  making his heart's desire a reality.
A young man of twenty two driving by himself
  stopping often, enjoying his journey to the West.
He chose to go to Riverside, California
  to work as a chemist in the field of Citrus.
He had heard about an extensive program
  at the university in their research department.
But upon arrival he learned the program and
  the department had been relocated to Hawaii.

So plan B was to go to the employment agency
with resume in hand to find himself a job.
It was a daunting experience, lots of paperwork
to be filled out, long lines, and interviews.
Choosing a particular line for his final interview
he handed his papers to a friendly looking lady.
Reading resume and noting where he'd come from
she couldn't contain her surprise exclaiming,
"Wow, not long ago I processed a resume from a
man also from the Dutch East Indies and Holland."
The young man's ears perked up and he begged the lady
to please give him the man's name and address.
Citing he was all by himself, knew no one in Riverside
and would love to connect with fellow countrymen.
The law did not permit her to comply with his request
but felt sorry for the young man as he longed a family.
Making her excuse to see about filing away papers
she left name and address in full view on her desk.
Jimmy clearly could see it was meant for him and gladly
pocketed the info while waiting for interview to end.
After the successful interview with the lady, he promptly
raced to his car and drove to the man's address.
And that is how Jimmy the young man came knocking
on our door that beautiful spring day and never left.

How amazing God is for having orchestrated such a wondrous thing!

This young man who had immigrated from Holland by himself was sponsored by a church in Hobbs, New Mexico. After just a couple of months working and living in New Mexico, this young man decided he wanted to try his luck finding a job in his field of chemistry in California. Of course, his sponsors tried to dissuade him from doing so as they were financially responsible for him for five years. And who would do that in California for him, they asked him. Did he perhaps know someone there that would or could? Where upon the young man replied, "No there is no one!"

Being stubborn about it, he persisted as his mind was made up. He made plans to venture out, packed up his car, said his good-byes, and with maps in hand and penciled routes, set out for the unknown. Determined to make this adventure the journey of his life, he allowed himself to see as much of America as he could. He went, saw and visited many beautiful national parks, vistas, and random spots he found on the way to California, knowing full well he might not get a chance like it anytime soon! Even going out of his way to remote areas to see, explore, and discover, sleeping in his tent or sometimes in his car. Enjoying nature and different landscapes in all its splendor and beauty. The spectacular sunsets and sunrises, the starry nights, the enormity of the heavens, the galaxies, the planetary formations, all of it. This young man Jimmy, till this day, looked upon this adventure, coming out West, as being the most precious and treasured gift.

When Jimmy arrived in Riverside, he got a temporary room at the YMCA and set out right away to see about a job he read about. It was for an experimental research project of citrus culture, in the chemistry department at UCR, only upon arrival did he find out that they had relocated the department to Hawaii. Plan B was to then go to an employment agency to find work, preferably in his field of food science.

Here we see God's hand upon Jimmy as he was directed to the specific waiting line with resume in hand to the woman who had just recently helped another man with approximately the same background and who had also come to America via Holland from the Dutch East Indies, my father!

Dear reader, what do you think were the chances of Jimmy and Meisje finding and meeting each other? What about the correlation of both being sponsored by churches in relatively small cities in different states with the same experiences and of the same heritage, that of being Eurasians? Coincidence? Accidental? Chance? Luck? Or is it Providence? God's hand?

Chapter 8

When Jimmy knocked on Meisje's front door, he felt so right at home he never wanted to leave. Jimmy got along fabulously with Meisje and her family and came to visit often. Many times, Jimmy would leave behind a sweater, a book, his camera, or whatever stuff he happened to have brought along thus having an excuse to return.

Pretty soon Jimmy was invited to live with Meisje's family as it was evident he longed for and thrived in a family setting. This invitation was heartily and enthusiastically accepted by Jimmy as well as Meisje and her siblings. Soon a friendship developed and blossomed as Jimmy settled in with the family. Discoveries were made of having mutual friends and several common interests as well, particularly between Jimmy and Meisje. They felt comfortable with each other and the common interests they had made the bond between them special as their friendship grew and they became closer.

Two years into their friendship the dynamics changed as Jimmy had fallen in love with Meisje. By this time Jimmy's parents and siblings had immigrated to America as well and had settled in San Diego, California, where they were sponsored. Both families got along splendidly and trips to each other's family ensued on a regular basis. It was on one of those trips to San Diego that, on the way back to Riverside, Jimmy popped the question and asked Meisje (me) if I wanted to be his "girl"—in the Dutch language he asked me to be his "Meisje." I was so taken back by that, startled, surprised, and even scared, yet nervously stammered, "YES!" and burst out in tears! We were in front of the house by then. He popped the question after a nervous last ten-minute car ride of closing and opening the car windows by Jimmy ... up and down ... up and down ... being very nervous, trying to get enough courage to pop the question! Poor guy!

Here is my poem "Meisje" that tells in more detail what transpired that fateful momentous day.

Meisje

Two years into our friendship the dynamics
of our relationship changed.
The stranger who had come knocking on our door
and who'd become a dear friend fell in love,
started to pursue, woo, and chase me.
Unbeknown to me, puzzled at the attention
and offers of rides in his car from school to work,
thinking it was all to lighten my daily schedule.
Accepting the sort of dating ritual, though one-sided
I got to know the caring compassionate Jimmy
whose love for parents and sisters ran deeply.
Six months later Jimmy asked my parents if he could
take me to San Diego … a couple of hours drive to
visit and spend time with his family and friends.
We had a wonderful time and started back home
early evening, enjoying the ride and beautiful
weather … winding roads 'n changing sceneries.
Close to home Jimmy started to get hot, so I thought,
for he kept turning the car window up and down
a couple of times and acting very nervous.
Stopping in front of our home I could see him
practically sweating, attempting to speak as he
blurted out … "DO YOU WANT TO BE MY GIRL?"
Startled and taken aback by his question, I shakenly
replied "Yes!" Opened the car door, ran with tears
streaming down my face, leaving a bewildered Jimmy.
Stepping inside our house running straight to the bedroom
falling into Mama's arms saying all the while, "I said 'Yes,'
I said 'Yes,' but I don't know why I said 'Yes,'" sobbing.
Shaken Mama searched my face trying to make some sense
of what could have happened. Ignoring the thoughts

that came rushing to her mind of the worst scenario.
Embraced in her arms rocking me ever so gently and
softly whispering sweet nothings in my ear ... calming
me down so I could tell her what had transpired.
By then Jimmy had come in to show his concern,
to explain and to join in, in our conversation, letting
Mama know it was definitely a one-sided "LOVE", his.
Then Mama told both of us that the day Jimmy had come
knocking on our door she knew that he would be the man
that was destined to marry her oldest daughter, me.
And so, it was that I became his "Meisje" girl that October,
a month later his fiancée, and almost a bride in December
if Jimmy had his way, but wedding came the year after.

As you can well imagine a lot of emotions and changes from that time on were experienced by Meisje. From friendship to being engaged was a huge adjustment as courtship was in full swing and Jimmy was requested to move out to find his own place to live till marriage! Jimmy chose the month of July for our wedding and decided to do it between our birthdays which would make it the twenty third of July. Three days after my birthday and three days before his! With that date penciled in on the calendar a flurry of activities ensued. Planning the wedding and all that pertains to it in less than a year, made the days seem to fly by even faster.

Meisje and her mother became very close as they planned, worked, sewed together, and bonded as women only can. Enjoying each other as Meisje was being prepped and instructed in the fine art of marriage. Here is a poem about the days leading up to the wedding.

Wedding/Honeymoon

Meisje's engagement brought a lot of changes.
For one, Jimmy had to move from being a boarder
in our home to his own rented room somewhere else.
Luckily, he found a place a couple houses down
across from our street which suited us just fine.
We decided on a July wedding date and had about
eight months to plan, find an apartment big enough
to accommodate us and a couple with a baby which
Jimmy had sponsored in addition to two bachelors.
Busy days ensued with college, work and helping at home
as Jimmy and Meisje started dating unchaperoned, often
going to San Diego to see Jimmy's family which gave
Meisje a chance to get to know him better as she watched
him lovingly interact and care for his parents and sisters.
Together with her Mama she designed a simple princess line
gown with a sweetheart neckline made from heavy satin,
ivory-colored with some appliques, a lace jacket with tapered
sleeves and tiny pearl buttons, an illusion veil held by
hand crafted flowers made from nylon stockings.
They also sewed all the bride maids' gowns, maid of honor's,
flower girl's and the ring bearer's suit comprising of black trousers,
matching black vest, white shirt, and black bow tie. They even
fashioned the flower bouquets and boutonnieres using
store bought flowers and incorporating garden greenery.
For Meisje this was a time of close bonding with her Mama
who taught and instructed her on life's lessons as a married
woman, wife, and eventually mother. Wishing her oldest
girl the most loving, happiest, harmonious married life ever.

Meisje remembers conversations on the intimacies of marriage being discussed as well as constructive and positive tips in strengthening a relationship based on trust, faithfulness, and forgiving one another, as being the key for making a marriage successful. Meisje also vaguely remembered the references her mother made to the hardships for maintaining those promises during WWII between her parents. Things her mother tried to explain that occurred during captivity in the concentration camp which she'd endured as a form of punishment. Meisje truly tried to process the horrific information related to her in secret in those times of bonding with Mama.

This was the first time Meisje could remember that some of the horror and atrocities during WWII which were perpetrated on and endured by Mama and witnessed by Meisje were mentioned. Although Meisje remembered a few times in Holland where Mama had battled PTSD episodes, one time resulting in a complete nervous breakdown to the point where Meisje had to step-in to take over the care of her siblings and household until a professional caregiver was assigned.

It's incredible, really, how for one's own preservation, one stores and files away those memories. That's a good thing too. Now looking back and remembering the things Mama shared, Meisje (I) could not have understood it until I became a mother myself. And when I did remember, it took a long, very long time, to even consider facing it and processing the horrific truth of the atrocities perpetrated on Mama. It took becoming a mother myself to understand.

Poor, poor Mama to have endured it by herself with no help or counseling or having shared it with another person who could have related to what she'd gone through. But it seems NO ONE from that generation talked about it nor shared it.

Chapter 9

Meisje and Jimmy enjoyed a typical and normal life like any other married couple in the 1960s. It was comprised of making a living and raising a family. They had two children a boy and a girl. A dream that became a reality was born out of a photograph seen in an American magazine a long time ago in Holland. Depicting a beautiful couple and their two children, a boy and a girl. As I write this, memories come to mind of Meisje, as a teenager, who had started dreaming, imagining, the beautiful couple and their children in Life magazine to be hers. Same as how she has dreamed about immigrating to America, seeing movie stars, cowboys and Indians, all having come to pass to her wonderment! Here is a poem about those dreams, longings and imaginings.

Dreams

Clickety clack, clickety clack, goes the train
Observing, scenery upon scenery, through the window
Excitement, anticipation, imagination, heart racing
Believe, believe, part of dream … now fulfilled!

Clickety clack, clickety clack, here I am
America, America, big, bold, the U S A
Movie stars, cowboys, Indians, Hollywood
Believe, believe, part of dream … California

Clickety clack, clickety clack, here I am
Riverside, Riverside, our home to be
Papa, Mama, kids, finally here, and me
Believe, believe, part of dream … fulfilled!

Dreams, dreams, do come true, imagine
Movie stars, cowboys, Indians, now a reality
Photograph of couple with son and daughter
Seen years ago, in Holland in an US magazine

Dreams, dreams, do come true, imagine
The Sherman Institute, school for Indians
Yearly Pow-wow, performances so spectacular
Mission Inn, frequented by movie stars in its glory days
Cowboys, cowhands on ranches and dairy farms
Photograph of family scene fulfilled, years later
Imagine, all in Riverside, California, America, U S A
DREAMS, dreams, do come true, IMAGINE!

Jimmy had several jobs before landing the job of his dreams at StarKist Tuna, where he got the chance to travel all over the world for twenty-eight years. And even after he was let go close to retirement, the company still retained him for several more years as a consultant. Meisje was a stay-at-home mom and only worked part-time in the evenings when it was needed to supplement their income. Only when the kids were older did she take a job working part-time in retail that gave her the flexibility of traveling with Jimmy whenever possible.

Looking back on those years, she remembers how fully she began to identify with Mama in many ways. In giving birth for instance, the struggles with illnesses, the finances, the ups and downs, the highs and lows of marriage. She particularly recalled a time, when her father called the family together telling them he had a SECRET to confess which he had sworn to uphold for twenty-five years. He vowed never to divulge the secret until after the twenty-five years had passed. And what a bombshell of a secret it was!

I remember Papa falling on his knees, asking Mama for forgiveness with tears streaming down his face. I remember the expression on Mama's face as slowly things that they had endured during their brutal captivity in the concentration camp came rushing in.

Papa's secret of having been recruited by the Americans to join their military intelligence in a highly secret covert operation was finally fully divulged to the family. Pieces of the missing puzzle came together bit by bit, though not all of it made sense, at least not to me at the time. But as Papa explained the Japanese had their own intelligence, the infamous brutal Kempeitai! When it was discovered that Papa worked with the American intelligence, they took him captive, shipped him to Japan and imprisoned him in a concentration camp where he was used as slave labor to work in a copper mine in Hidachi. Hence his family was taken and imprisoned as well, with the plan that the Kempeitai could extort from Mama the "truth."

How Meisje reacted to Papa asking her personally for forgiveness was well-noted and acknowledged. As I vaguely remember, filing and storing that memory right away, deep into my soul, as unsettled feelings and other memories came to the surface in my mind. Things that made me feel a heavy and profound sadness in my heart and spirit for Papa, as for all of us too, as he tried to convey and justify the hardships he endured as well.

Papa explained how the ship he was transported on to Japan had been torpedoed by mistake, the American allies not realizing that there were allies taken as prisoners on that Japanese ship. Papa was thrown into the air and landed in the ocean. He grabbed a piece of the wreckage and climbed on it with a couple other survivors. With a stoic face, Papa told how he and the others survived at sea for several days, and then were rescued, but to their horror by the enemy, the Japanese. They were then shipped to Japan where he was imprisoned as a prisoner of war.

Papa also told how he had seen a glow in the distance of the atomic bomb when it was dropped by the Americans, and the euphoric and happiness the prisoners felt of finally having HOPE return as they celebrated VICTORY and awaited their rescue and liberation.

Here is a poem I wrote about Papa's service during the war which I titled "Secret," appropriately so.

Secret

A young husband, father, and teacher now serving the Military.
  Fighting the Japanese, defending the Dutch East Indies islands
    for Holland.
      Was recruited by the Americans into their Intelligence Service,
        a highly covert
          operation swearing an oath not to divulge the
          secret until 20-25 yrs. after the war!

All unbeknownst to his family to only be captured shortly thereafter
  by counter intelligence and sent by ship to Japan.
    Then bombed by friendly
      fire not too long into their journey, clinging onto a piece
      of ship wreckage for days!
        Wounded, cold, and hungry, fighting the elements trying
        to survive the ordeal!

And then finally to be rescued and having "happiness" be only short-lived
  and bitter sweet for it was the Japanese who fished him
    and two of his mates out of the sea
      to continue the transport further to Japan. Knowing full well
        what he would face
          as a POW could be horrendous hardship, he was extremely
          grateful to be alive!

Captured, seized, and put to hard labor in a copper mine he promised himself
  to stay alive no matter what! Had he known this would be
    by far the ultimate test
      for survival he would face, he might not have made
      that pledge to himself.
        Three long years of unspeakable HORROR, *slave labor,*
        hunger, punishment, and torture!

AMERICANS ... ATOM BOMBS ... LIBERATED

Note: Papa survived the years in captivity and slave labor in the copper mine and was liberated in 1945. He was reunited with his family in 1946. How that happened was so miraculous as well, dear ones. I will share that part a bit later!

Chapter 10

After that secret bombshell was divulged, Papa finally felt a release like a big burden was lifted off his shoulders. On the other hand, for Mama and Meisje it was the opposite. (And perhaps for Meisje's other siblings as well. They didn't speak of it at the time, so Meisje didn't know for sure.) Now they each had to try in their own way to process how to fit and put together the missing pieces of the puzzle which they'd carried and wondered about for so long.

For Meisje it took many, many years trying to sort out and put bits and pieces together to have it all make some sense. Quite often for Meisje, pieces of the puzzle would come through incidents seen, heard, or experienced over the years. Yet still there remained a shroud of secrecy, a mystery, especially pertaining to the covert operation Papa was involved in. Meisje was not able to understand or get more information. Meisje never obtained exact data either as she did not know how. Sadly, many things stayed unclear for Papa was not voluntarily sharing, he was unwilling to do so. It was too traumatic for him to recall, relive, and tell.

Meisje learned a lot more about WWII over the past couple of years through reading history books on WWII in the Pacific theater and biographies as well. In particular, there were two movies she saw that were especially enlightening, one called *Unbroken* and the other *The Railway Man.*

Meisje finds it so sad that not much about the war in that region is exposed, found, or reported. Because there actually is plenty of historical evidence that was reported, filmed, photographed, written and recorded about this period of history, but for some reason it is being left out. Even the schools neglect to teach on the subject or carry books on it in their libraries. This, in comparison to WWII in the European theater and the atrocities perpetrated there, particularly pertaining to the Holocaust.

Yet the war in the Pacific theater started in a horrific way, the sneak attack on Pearl Harbor by the Japanese in December 1941. This brought America into war in that region which expanded their involvement in Meisje's homeland, the Dutch East Indies in 1942, helping the Dutch fight the Japanese invasion to the islands and Meisje's father's recruitment by the Americans to join their intelligence in a highly secretive covert operation.

There is no comparison to say which war was worse than the other yet it took a consented decision to end the war in the Pacific theater by dropping the atomic bomb. This is what finally stopped the years and years of inhumane atrocities perpetrated by the Japanese and forced them to capitulate, thereby saving millions of lives.

There is much documentations and stories of the incredibly cruel torture that the Japanese guards put their captors through. Systematic starvation, waterboarding, hard/physical forced labor, sweat boxes, slapping, kicking, beatings, and solitary confinement in dug-out holes. Some prisoners of war were transported in bamboo pig baskets and then thrown into the sea, drowning them alive. Female prisoners were often raped and kept as sex slaves. Group punishments meted out consisted mostly of being forced to stand or stay in a bowed position in rows upon rows of prisoners for hours and hours in the unprotected elements of the tropics, whether it be the blazing sun or torrential rains.

The decision to drop the atomic bomb was a horrific decision indeed but necessary for Japan would never have capitulated! It is not in their character nor culture to do so. They would have to commit suicide—called Hara-kiri, in which they might shoot themselves or stab themselves to death with their sword, or cut their throat with their own knife. Military aviators may fly their planes kamikaze style, using it as a weapon to gladly and willingly sacrifice their lives in order to save face.

For us prisoners and countless others, the dropping of the ATOMIC BOMB meant FREEDOM, HOPE, LIBERATION, LIFE, and for those who were barely alive, it meant a second chance at LIVING—a gift granted to Papa, a POW concentration camp survivor of Japan. And for Mama, Meisje, and her siblings, it was also the most amazing precious gift, of having been liberated from Hell, a concentration camp so named by those who survived it. Although sadly, for many it came too late as their weakened, tortured, wasted bodies, and the many horrific atrocities they had endured, succumbed to death anyways on the day of liberation, or before that day or shortly thereafter.

Meisje too experienced group punishment. One time was because another prisoner failed to salute their captor and flag by not bowing to it. Here is a poem about that memory titled "Japanese Flag!"

Japanese Flag!

Rows and rows of women and children
in bowing position, in the heat of the day!
How longer must it be? So many are swaying
trying to hold that position to avoid beatings!
Punishment and so-called lessons were these exercises for not
showing honor and respect to the Japanese captors and their flag!

Finally, after hours upon hours the dismissal to go
to their quarters came as they held up one another!
With triumph in their eyes and a smile on their faces
for having endured another hardship successfully!
Unbeknownst to our captors the Dutch flag had waved proudly
by clothes worn in Red, White, Blue, and a bit of Orange!

One becomes very resourceful and imaginative in captivity
shown by the women in the front row, that we could stay loyal!
Paying homage to our own culture and heritage without compromising
even though oftentimes at a cost, to one's own life and discomfort!
Pain, suffering, torture, punishment in many forms inflicted daily was
common and manifested in starvation, illnesses, brokenness, and death!

Survival and staying alive with integrity was a daily struggle. Hopelessness, brokenness in mind, body, and soul forces one to either look inward or upward!

Chapter 11

Meisje sits on the deck of her dream house overlooking the aqua-blue ocean, still a bit shaky and breathless as she gazes out to sea. Thanking the good Lord, feeling blessed as she put her Bible, devotional, and journal down, reminding herself again and again of God's promise. She thought back to having woken up from another nightmare that morning. Knowing deep in her heart that God only would have her remember and retain what her mind could handle, she had allowed the nightmare to continue its course in order to recall, remember, and to write it down.

Oh, dear one, what a precious gift this is, knowing God is with me and letting me release what has been stored, filed, and I thought even been wiped out, deleted as it were from my mind. Indeed, God's mercy and goodness gives me the strength to face it. Allowing me to retain what I can handle thereby healing me, restoring me, and making me whole again. That is so incredibly amazing!

Meisje is doing a lot of poetry writing now, which is good therapy as well as speaking by invitation, sharing her story and several of her poems besides "America's Gift." She's also been interviewed several times and her story published in local newspapers and in several periodicals.

One poem that Meisje shares which touches many people, especially veterans, is "A Papa Photograph." This is the story of her family's miraculous reunion with Papa! Being freed for the second time was an exhilarating feeling for Meisje and her family. After WWII was over and Meisje and her mom and siblings were liberated from the camp, they were then captured again and whisked away. This time their captivity was by the Indonesian people who were fighting for their independence from the Dutch during the Bersiap (civil war).

While Papa had been looking for us as soon as he came back from Japan in 1946, on this particular day our paths miraculously crossed as we were transported to another city to reunite with Mama's family for a temporary stay. The miracle occurred as a jeep with military men headed the opposite way, crossed with our truck at a point where both vehicles had to slow down because the road had narrowed in a bend. That's when a jubilant little voice screamed, as my sister, the baby, now a four-year-old pointed her finger at a man in the jeep, recognizing him as the Papa photograph.

What a splendid reunion as we heard a screeching noise and saw the jeep come to an abrupt halt, turn around, and saw a skinny man in uniform run toward our truck. We heard Mama yell, "STOP!" as the truck came to a sudden standstill. We saw a joyous sister jump in the outstretched arms of our Papa, as Mama and the rest of us looked on in disbelief, for Mama had received word from the Red Cross that Papa had died during the war when he was torpedoed at sea.

This is one of the pieces of the puzzle Meisje is trying to put together, which is so hard to do because of Papa's secret intelligence covert operation and his twenty years of sworn oath not to divulge this information.

Here is a poem describing the event in more detail, dear one.

A Papa Photograph

Every evening she would gather
her children close to her
wrap them in her arms
and talk about their Papa.
Why he was not around
and what a wonderful man
he is, and soon, very soon
would see them again.
She believed with all her heart
the hardships they were enduring
in the concentration camp
was all but a temporary thing.

Though she herself was gone often
working as a "slave laborer" in a
factory and who knows where else
was very present when around.
Her children especially the baby
when gathered under her wings
as it were like a mother hen
would bask in her love and care.
She loved singing to them and
telling bedtime stories, ending with
passionate goodnight kisses planted
firmly on the Papa photograph.
Never in her wildest dream
could she have known
her fervent prayer and hope
the children not forget their father ...
Would soon be realized after the
war ended and her tortured body, soul,
and mind were rewarded for the rituals
she faithfully executed each evening.
For indeed a wondrous miracle unfolded
as the baby now a four-year-old
recognized and pointed to a man
in a jeep passing by our army truck
as her Papa photograph.
Materialized in the flesh
the baby who never knew a father
finally experienced the raptured rush of
throwing herself in the outstretched arms
to feel the love and warmth of
the beating heart of her Papa
as he hugged her close to him!

This poem is dedicated to my sister with much love and gratitude, for having recognized Papa and for being an overcomer and a survivor.

I still find it amazing the impact that those nightly rituals had and the wondrous joy it produced. People often come to me after a speaking engagement and particularly after having recited A Papa Photograph poem. It seems to touch people's hearts. How fortunate we are nowadays with the technology we have. With just a click of a button, kids can see their Papa or Mama and vice versa of course. The ones deployed can see and stay in touch with loved ones and even talk live via this wondrous media called Skype. Such a wonderful invention, don't you think?

Meisje and her siblings only had a tiny photograph of their Papa in a small locket on Mama's necklace to remember him by with nightly goodnight kisses performed on the photograph, all done in secret and with fear of being caught by guards patrolling nearby, which always made the rituals anxious moments! No wonder Meisje developed issues in later life, all stemming from the war years!

Thinking about this poem, Meisje remembers the condition they were forced to live in. No beds or cots to sleep on, only the bare floor where we huddled on woven straw mats with a blanket, which Mama had secured by bartering some jewelry at great risk of being caught.

When we were brutally taken to prison, Mama had very little time to pack. Fortunately, the first couple of nights we slept on some of our clothing which Mama had the foresight of bringing along. Mama used a few pieces for temporary bedding on the hard, bare concrete floor; except the baby who had the pillow for a mattress that Mama had brought along for that very purpose.

I still marvel and often wonder how Mama could have secured certain items for so many of our needs that arose during our captivity. Stilling our constant hunger was always her main concern. It became a big priority as how to supplement our meager handful of rice that was meted out daily; especially as the days, weeks, and months turned into years.

In the beginning, prisoners willingly shared their meager acquired and found foods. But all too soon it became a matter of one's own preservation because of the danger of being found out or caught. Others snitched for instance or one may be caught bartering for food by the fence, or God forbid, get caught stealing it. For if you were caught having secured even a little bit of food, a piece of fruit, a banana, a tomato or whatever, punishment would be meted out guaranteed, no matter what. It was such a sad thing to see people reduced to animal-like behavior, fighting just to stay alive. Hunger to the point of starvation will bring out the worst in people. Sometimes, even to the point of selling one's very own soul.

Truly the situation for the prisoners became so desperate as the years went by that foraging for food became an obsession. Anything edible was considered a go and soon we even resorted to eating grasshoppers and crickets which when roasted tasted very good. We also ate frogs, but only certain ones for some people died because some frogs were poisonous.

Brother managed to catch birds once in a while with his slingshot, even if they were small, big, it did not matter, all types of critters became coveted treats. Speaking of treats, a bar of soap was a coveted luxury, a prized item. It was often divided into smaller pieces for bartering, selling, or exchange. Hygiene became a big problem due to lack of toiletries. Can you imagine no shampoo for your hair? Or not even having toothpaste or a tooth brush? I remember if we had some toothpaste, how frugally it was used, only a smidgen of it applied on our finger or on Mama's finger to use as a brush to clean our teeth!

No wonder lack of hygiene created problems, such as infestation of mice, rats, ticks, and fleas broke out in the camp and soon was prevalent everywhere. Mama discovered to her horror, there were little white eggs in our hair and upon closer examination discovered we were covered with lice. She tried to combat it with all kinds of homemade remedies concocted out of whatever could be found but to no avail.

She was even able to secure a special comb for the lice removal. It had ridged tooth edges to scrape off the white eggs laid by the lice imbedded on the strings of our hair. What a nightmare that was, painful itching and constant scratching causing bleeding, wounds, and scabs. Only DDT powder applied with a pump and sprayed all over our head killed the lice. That was done by the Red Cross when we were liberated when we finally received a medical checkup.

For many of the prisoners, it was the first health examination since incarceration. For many, this was a much-needed health care benefit, finally provided by the Red Cross and a Godsend for all the ailments endured and contracted during captivity due to lack of food, nutrition, vitamins, medicine, and hygiene. Many of us came down with beriberi, a vitamin B deficiency inflicting the central nervous system, causing weight loss and difficulty in walking.

Scurvy, malaria, dysentery, eye infections, bronchial, and lung problems like tuberculosis were also common. Many of us suffered from edema, a horrible swelling of the extremities as well as the aforementioned head lice infestation.

Dear ones, can you see after reading this how Meisje treasures and cherishes even the very so called mundane things of life which often is taken for granted until it has been taken away, in her case, stripped away and denied?

Indeed, as Meisje sits on her deck, overlooking the ocean in her dream home, she reminds herself again multiple times, how very blessed she is to be alive and well. And to be so fortunate as to have a home so beautifully furnished with the luxuries afforded her. With cupboards filled to the brim, a refrigerator stocked with an array of foods, a bed and a pillow to sleep on! The luxury of showers, baths, and even a beautiful Spanish-tiled spa pool outside in the inner courtyard.

Surrounded by beautiful foliage, blooming orchids, roses, and many other flowers, bushes and trees. The sound of a flowing water fountain, the chirping and happy tweeting of birds in the trees, humming birds fluttering, hovering, drinking the nectar from the flowers and from the sweet liquid provided them in the hanging bottle feeders! Oh, my, life is sweet! Meisje noting, observing, drinking all this in, letting it seep deep within her mind as it soothes her soul and refreshes her body!

Meisje, oh so grateful, appreciative and thankful, feeling blessed beyond measure, her cup full to the brim overflowing with gratitude, singing praises to her heavenly Father.

Chapter 12

So often when I reflect back on the hardships endured during captivity, I can see how it has shaped and formed me into the person I have become. I am a product of the lessons learned from my past, from the struggles to stay alive and well—both physically and mentally. Lessons learned from adapting and making do with the resources on hand, sharpening one's wits using our imagination, becoming very cunning, always careful.

Trust, hunger, and safety were major issues and daily concerns to tackle, overcome, combat, and conquer. Being left alone when Mama was taken at night or sometimes during the day, not knowing where to, or understanding why, or when she will be back. All of that caused Meisje to grapple with angst and anxiety issues which through counseling were dealt with and labeled as abandonment issues and PTSD. Thank God for counseling and the help I received.

Oftentimes one hears or sees that someone has become a hoarder, some extreme, others not as much. I believe this stems from the war years or another traumatic event and not having enough. Keeping, holding on to things, never throwing out or giving away—afraid, after all you never know when you might need it. Hence, saving or hoarding things becomes a habit, good or bad, and depending on the severity, it becomes a sickness. No wonder, dear one, that one can either become "bitter" or "better" in life after having gone through captivity, don't you think?

I don't know about others, but in my case, I became so aware of the lack and the absence of things that later on "everything" became precious to me, from material things, to freedom, to the simple ordinary pleasures in life! Mesje (I) see beauty in everything, cherish and treasure all that I have, and don't take anything for granted. Others who know Meisje always comment on how artistic she is and how beautifully her interior home is designed. She's also known for keeping a very organized and clean home. So true! This all stems from having to do without and having to live in squalor conditions in the concentration camp and all during WWII and Bersiap civil war.

Let me tell you, dear one, no matter how poor or well-off Meisje was, how small or how big her home was, she always knew how to make it livable and beautiful very inexpensively. She also likes to surround herself with books for she's an avid reader; flowers and plants for she enjoys gardening and also has a flair for floral design. She also likes to draw and paint and often incorporates her creations by displaying them throughout her home. She loves music and songs, especially classical, though she does not play an instrument nor has a good voice.

That's enough information on Meisje (me), I just wanted to show how much a product of the war years I became and came away with and the difference it can make. All I can share with you, dear one, is how I've dealt with my issues stemming from the war years and incarceration, and the choices I have made to overcome it successfully. Which is still an ongoing process I might add. But I'm doing it with much gratitude, thanksgiving, and appreciation for all the opportunities thrown, landed, sown, seized on my life's path so as to capture the most beautiful journey here on earth!

Oftentimes we value things only after we've lost it or don't have it anymore. That's why I have also come to treasure relationships, due to the fact that my Papa was taken away from me at a very young age; not comprehending or processing the how, what, why and where, traumatized me as did also the uncertainty of Mama's nightly disappearances. The angst, fear, and anxieties of such losses, for however long or short of a duration, made me treasure and cherish the times Mama was around me and present.

Later reuniting with Papa, the joy was so euphoric, dear one, akin to seeing the joy and happiness of children and families now anxiously awaiting the return of their loved ones from Afghanistan, Iraq, Iran, or from wherever in the world. That's why relationships, friendships, families, and friends are everything to me; it means the world to me and I don't take it for granted. I pride myself on nourishing, maintaining, loving, caring and nurturing a relationship, for that is what it takes for a relationship to thrive, blossom, and be successful. It takes two of course, for it to work, but by putting in all that work, it is well worth the effort. To me, friendships and relationships are prized treasures that ought to be cherished, for they are so precious, and not ever to be taken for granted.

At a very young age, confronted daily with the deaths of fellow captives, Meisje learned how fragile life can be, knowing full well that tomorrow is not guaranteed and yesterday is no more, leaving us with today which is called the "present," appropriately so, for it is a treasured gift indeed! That's why looking back at the hardships endured, I can see how God lovingly and graciously protected Meisje. I believe God preserved her for "such a time as this" (Esther 4:14b) for clearly "God has a plan and a purpose" (Jer. 29:11) for Meisje all along, and that is to share her memories in a memoir with all her loved ones and others.

Here are two poems that I want to share with you about my brother at a young age and the other about another young boy. You will see as you read, how circumstances made them play an adult role at a very young age, a role they felt was their duty to do so. My love and admiration for them, I will carry in my heart forever, for their actions greatly impacted my life.

I titled one "Brother, My Hero," which I've dedicated to my older brother in gratitude for all he did for us at such a young age. The other one is called "Brave Young Heart, "which impacted me spiritually, for I recognize now that "seeds" were planted and came to fruition years later as I accepted Christ as an adult at the age of thirty-one years.

Brother, My Hero

Born at the height of our parent's wealth
and raised as a prince with splendor
With our hearts desires, at our command
*   we enjoyed a privileged life.*
All that changed in a heartbeat
*   when world war two broke out*

And were taken from comfort and luxury
  to a deplorable concentration camp.
We were imprisoned for 3 1/2 years
  and systematically punished
By starvation and lack of medical services
  clearly in violation of the Geneva Convention.
Our mother did her best to provide
  by bartering or pawning jewelry
You brother, felt responsible, being the man
  as young as you were, and took charge.
Every day you would go hunting
  sling-shot in hand, scavenging food
Trying not to come back empty-handed,
  a bird instead of crickets was the goal.
Punishment born by you by our captors
  when you succeeded was the price paid
As we feasted, weakened by such hunger
  knowing what you endured to secure it.
My heart is full of gratitude and no words
  can express the love and admiration
I have for you, displaying such selflessness
  and hardship as a boy, caring for us all

Brave Young Heart

A chance meeting with
  a young boy and his bravery
    in the concentration camp
Witnessed on a daily basis
  for some three plus years
    impacted many of us.
Enduring extreme hardship
  Systematic starvation
    And daily punishments
      Inflicted by the guards
        For all kinds of infractions

He remained such a source
of Joy for his Mama and others
with his upbeat personality
always smiling and whistling
no matter what.
Rumors had it
he has no father
Although he himself claimed
God as his heavenly Father
and being the King's son
Refusing there for
the ritual of bowing
that our Japanese captors
insisted on and demanded.
This young boy
was most assuredly
doomed for more hardship
than any of us.
Thus began the daily
beatings and torture
trying to break him
after every refusal.
But always he came back
seemingly fine, in good spirits
and with incredible grace
though his eyes betrayed
the pain he'd suffered.
Until the day, close to the end
of our imprisonment
An announcement came
for all to assemble
in the courtyard
to witness his execution.
Row upon row of women
and children gathered

Bowing to our captors
were told this was a lesson
Then the order to fire
upon the young boy was given
and the command
for us to watch.
Several bullets hit his body
yet standing he remained
as if someone was
holding him up.
His Mama and others pleaded
for him to bow
but to no avail
Until the soldiers
shot his kneecaps
and down he went
Willing himself to keep
his head up
with pain and sadness
mirrored in his eyes
for his captors
he finally succumbed
Falling to the ground
joy and peace
bathed his face
As his soul left
the crumpled, bullet-
riddled body
Rushing to meet the
outstretched arms
of his heavenly Father.

Almost immediately
after darkness, despair,
shock, and disbelief
settled around us

Instantaneously flooding in
  came a light of pure mercy
    piercing the hearts
      of many.
Still standing awestricken
  by this miraculous gift
    this young boy left
      to ponder the meaning
        of such uncompromising faith
For all to either
  accept or reject
    God's wondrous sacrificial
      gift of the CROSS!

My brother had a hard time processing the atrocities he witnessed and that were perpetuated upon him, especially near the end of WWII. As a matter of fact, for his own preservation his mind would shut down. He would blackout, fall down, and start foaming at the mouth, his body turning, twisting, jerking, in spasm-like movements, akin to that of epileptic seizures.

Mama taught me how to help with brother's seizures so he'll not injure himself, by inserting the handle of a spoon in his mouth. After the war when we lived in Holland the doctors there, diagnosed him with having Epilepsy. It was not until we were here in America and brother was examined and underwent a lot of tests and x-rays, that the doctors concluded the condition he had was sustained due to trauma. His mind at such a young age, seeing, and witnessing atrocities plus the slapping and blows to the head contributed to the brain trauma injuries.

Tests performed with electrodes to the brain and other tests measured abnormalities, indicating trauma sustained similar to that of a POW with severe PTSD. Well, brother certainly was traumatized during WWII and during the Bersiap, as was I, except that I processed my trauma differently. I hid mine in my subconscious, buried it deep down in my soul, imagined it away to also stay sane I guess, or rather self-preservation. Also, I suppressed it, due to being too young to have understood the severity. Or because I couldn't grasp the gravity of such evilness. Brother, who was older than I, understood better, nevertheless, was hugely traumatized by what he had seen, heard, witnessed, and experienced.

One particular horrendous incident happened after our liberation from the WWII camp, but we were locked up again, this time under the Indonesians during their civil war. Our servant, who we called Babu, had heard we had been freed, and been looking for us, found us imprisoned again and decided to help. She came by one night to sneak us food and was caught doing so by the guards and witnessed by Mama and brother. I was awoken by piercing screams, yelling, and a lot of commotion as our dear Babu's hands were chopped off! What a horrific nightmare!

You can well imagine how traumatizing that was for all of us, especially since this happened to someone we knew and loved—our Babu! Poor Babu, who felt sorry for us, was concerned about our weakened condition, and only wanted to help and did so out of the goodness of her heart. She was punished by her own people's law, for Muslim law requires "an eye for an eye, a tooth for a tooth."

In our servant's case, Babu's hands did the "offense" therefore it had to be dealt with by chopping it off. If it were her tongue, her tongue would had been pulled out; if it were her eyes they would have no problem gouging out her eyes. Very harsh laws, indeed, but nevertheless a reality that they live by.

We never found out what happened to our dear servant. I hope to thank her one day, either here on earth or in heaven, for what she so selflessly did and at such a high price and cost.

Can you imagine, dear one, what it does to one's mental state to eat the food then that was brought in under these conditions? All during captivity one undergoes mixed feelings about food, being hungry all the time one would feast, gorge on food, knowing very well the risk if caught. So sad, it took Meisje (me) a long time to be able to "enjoy" eating food without feeling "guilt" of the consequences associated with it.

Another impactful incident I witnessed in the concentration camp and wrote about is the poem *Brave Young Heart*. This young boy was separated from his Mama early on into captivity when he reached the age of thirteen years and was transferred to a men's camp next door to ours. Somehow, he always managed to sneak back into our camp to see his Mama, to give her extra food and to check on her well-being. He full well knew the risk and the cost, because guaranteed some type of punishment was always the price he would pay for those deeds.

Also he refused to bow to our captors and the Japanese flag. This was a daily ritual that the Japanese guards demanded and any defiance was seen as a severe sign of disobedience and disrespect.

I think the biggest impact this young boy had on me was his Christian belief. For me (Meisje), his very being, his conduct, and the hardship he endured were "seeds" of faith sown in my life, not only during captivity but all throughout my journey. For it was in this concentration camp Banyu Biru, in Ambarawa, that I, Meisje, was introduced to God at a very young age. By those who cursed Him on a daily basis and by those who called on Him daily.

So yes, definitely this brave young boy who was executed at around age sixteen or seventeen impacted me spiritually and I presume for others as well. I'm sure for those who call themselves believers, he was a role model, one to emulate and to learn from his uncompromising stance.

You know, dear one, I know personally some who have survived the war and come through their ordeal victorious and others who became very bitter people and ended up having miserable lives to the day they died. I find that so very sad; for not being able to forgive and let go, they were then "victimized" twice for carrying all their baggage from the war years with them! THIS PAINS ME! Being a victim once is enough punishment in my opinion. That is why I advocate and opt for counseling for myself and anyone else. Better not become a victim again by staying victimized. I've tried to rise above it and not give my captors of so long ago the satisfaction of "victory" by bringing it with me. It's easier said than done, dear ones, for sure. Hats off to those that can and could do it and have accomplished it.

I'm grateful that nowadays those who've served or have gone to war get the help they need. We should always encourage them to seek not only medical help for their physical wounds but also seek help for their mental and psychological well-being. I also highly recommend spiritual help. I discovered and know now that a person is comprised of three components—body, mind, soul. For best functioning and success, all three parts need to be in perfect balance and harmony to each other.

Sickness in just one of the three components, even if it is minor, causes imbalance and will need adjustment. In other words, when you hurt physically, it will affect the mind as well as your spirit. If you're mentally ill for example, depressed, it often disables you physically (no energy), plus robs you of hope (spirit), and takes away what little faith you have, if any.

If you're hurting spiritually, you've lost hope or faith, can't see a way out, etc., and you don't strengthen your spiritual side, replenish it, bring harmony, and peace of mind, then the mind and body will suffer big time as well, even if you don't recognize that is what's going on. I believe we're all aware of having these three components. Sadly, most take care of only the body and mind and ignore or completely do away with the spirit/soul. I would be remiss if I did not share that part with you, dear one. For me, the soul or spirit is very important; without it there is no joy in my life. For that "joy" in my case represents the Lord and is the Lord. And the Lord is my "joy" and my "strength" Amen!

There is a moral compass that measures and registers one's conscience, if that has been injured and physically traumatized, through therapy and counseling one can be healed. I find it amazingly wonderful that there's now research being done in that particular area of the spirit/soul/conscience. I applaud the work being done, especially with the veterans.

Healing the "spirit" is a relatively new concept, for it does call for one to forgive in order to move on—forgiveness for oneself or another person(s). This type of trauma to the conscience has been defined as "moral injury" by the psychiatric field. Moral injury is a wound to the soul, the spirit. In my case, in order to move forward I needed to forgive, which is not an easy thing to do.

You often find these types of wounds and injuries in soldiers who have killed and witnessed killings or seen horrific torture, or those who have been sexually abused. Or it might be for those who have experienced some kind of trauma of some sort—a trauma due to loss. A loss of a loved one through death for instance, caused either by illness, accident, miscarriage, or abortion. All very traumatic. As is the loss in divorce, loss of a job, home, finances, etc.

These wounds, injuries, scars inflicted to the soul, the spirit, are invisible but cut deep and are extremely painful. These wounds now have a name. It is a moral injury to the soul, the spirit. Treatment for it varies, in my case, I opted to work with "forgiveness" as I found this to be the only way possible for moving forward. Forgiveness is the best medicine for healing, so to speak, for either another or for oneself. I will go into more detail on that subject later when I introduce you to my friend, Corrie.

Now, before I get too far along in my story, let me share my poem titled "Babu" with you so you can see more easily why I've struggled with survivor's guilt in addition to abandonment issues and other disorders, dear one.

Babu

Remembering Babu our dear Indonesian servant.
Hired for household chores and for looking after
us kids as well.
She loved us dearly and according
to Mama would spoil us with special treats!
As I ponder why she comes to mind,
I shove her gently back into the recesses of my mind
as I fall back to resume my sleep.
Yet not long after I wake up with a start again …
heart racing … as I hear my husband
whisper, "A nightmare dear?" as I nod my head in
agreement and clutch the top of my nightgown …
shivering as my chest heaves up and down …
trying to calm myself … as memories of Babu surface …
and I stifle my screams falling back on my pillow.
Scenes come to mind … questions and conversations

I had with Mama years later ... not comprehending, denial.
Tucking memories back deep into my consciousness ...
what Mama told me had happened to Babu ... witnessed and
seen by us so long ago!
I let myself remember certain things ...
little by little I process what I can handle ... as
horror, pain, sadness, survivor's guilt,
gratitude for our Babu vividly come to mind ...
vowing to myself to thank her when I meet her in heaven ...
for surely she deserves the best place in God's Kingdom for her
selfless act!
Oh, God how much did she suffer
for sneaking food to where we were held imprisoned?
I still hear her SCREAMS!
I still remember Mama telling me the guards
"CHOPPED OFF HER HANDS!"

MUSLM LAW, SHE KNEW THE DANGER, THE COST, YET SHE RISKED!

As you can imagine, survivor's guilt is an extremely difficult emotion to get over. It is a psychological condition that people find themselves in when they have survived traumatic events while others did not. How I dealt with it was such a long process and took years and years to overcome. I, Meisje, was able to forgive her Japanese and Indonesian captors, but forgiving herself took a long time and a lot of help. Guilt for being alive, realizing the cost, the blood that was spilled, the price of one's life being offered for freedom, is way too high a cost especially if death is the price to be paid.

Forgiving oneself is always harder, as I have lived with guilt for being alive at the expense of someone else's sacrifices or death. It's such a huge thing to process! As I grew older and became an adult, a married woman, a mother, now a grandma, I came to understand the consequences of war. Just thinking of the masses of young men and women willingly being sent out to fight for the freedom of countries and its people is mind boggling to me.

Liberating people for that very purpose, helping them, freeing them from captivity, atrocities, and possible death. Doing it sacrificially at such a huge risk to their own safety. Putting themselves in harm's way, getting wounded, sometimes ending up losing limbs, or God forbid sacrificing their own lives. Yet that happens. Some people come back not only physically wounded, but mentally and emotionally as well as spiritually scarred. Knowing all that and becoming so aware of the COST, the price that was paid on my behalf, it weighs heavily on my mind and in my heart, and in my spirit.

Hence, the survivor's guilt. I can't imagine my son or daughter, or a grandchild of mine fighting, risking their lives and possibly even being killed for the freedom of a foreigner, God forbid! Or liberating them from atrocities, poverty, and oppression. Believe me, it's a huge price, a tremendous cost that was paid for my freedom. So many, many people have died for me, a foreigner, why, why, WHY?

Oh, dear one, I am so aware of it because I am the recipient of this beautiful gift. Although I have accepted this gift and have been able to move on, I don't know for sure if the guilt of being alive has completely dissipated. When I'm confronted with the guilt, it's replaced right away with so much gratitude for the gift of sacrifice that it becomes bearable to live with. I now see the guilt as akin to that of a deep wound that's healed and is now a scar, embedded with an imprint, stamped, infused, with much gratitude, lots of thanksgiving and tremendous love! Truly my cup runneth over! I have such a deep abiding love for all who so willingly serve. I've promised to always show my gratitude by thanking them personally through my speaking engagements and through my writing, and through sharing my poem *America's Gift*, a tribute to our service men and women. I think such an amazing love deserves God's amazing blessings, don't you agree dear hearts?

This gift of freedom is one that truly is an ongoing gift. It is the gift that keeps on giving. I say that because I think of how I have benefited from the sacrifice of America's soldiers, my family, as immigrants to the US in the 1950s benefited. Jimmy and his family as immigrants benefited. And now, my children, the two of them, with their spouses and children, my four grandchildren have benefited. Yes, freedom is the gift that keeps on giving.

I have visited many American graves in cemeteries around the world with my hubby. Truly, oftentimes one has no clue (and certainly I did not either), as to how many soldiers have died or have sacrificed, given their lives for country, family, friends, strangers, foreigners. Why? After many years and having met many veterans through my speaking engagements, did I find out WHY? One word, and that word is FREEDOM.

Dear one, I am a recipient of that freedom, fought on battlefields, gained for me on foreign soil far away by masses of sons and daughters sent by America to secure that precious gift called freedom.

What is Freedom? Well, to me, freedom means to not have someone dictate to me when to speak or eat, when I should bathe, sleep, or awaken; when I can go to school, work, or play; can laugh, dance, sing, or read. Oh, dear one, when these simple pleasures are taken away, in my case during my incarceration in the concentration camp, are no more, I am not free. It means I've lost my freedom. You know in some countries, there is no freedom to do these simple pleasures. There are restrictions on freedom, either in a mild form, or severe, and mostly geared toward women.

Women who have no say or choice in their clothing. They are forced to cover themselves from head to toe except for the eyes. They call those dresses Burkas. God forbid if some body part is accidentally exposed, that calls for a beating, deserving or not, it does not matter. Also, in some countries, women are denied an education. Some women have no freedom to choose their own mates and can be forced into marriage as early as ten years old or younger. How horrible is that? I'm sure you have heard stories like this as well. Can you believe that sort of thing is still happening in this day and age?

Ah, freedom, how we take it for granted. Did you know in some European countries one cannot just move from one place to another? This is because you must register in each city that you live. One must ask permission from the city government to move, check out, and reregister in the new city. Thank God, that is not so here in the USA. We have freedom of movement, wherever we want to go or can afford to. We also have freedom of speech. We are allowed to express ourselves in whatever media, be it written or oral. This is not so in some other countries, for one can be jailed for speaking or expressing one's mind. I'm so glad we have freedom of speech, as well as of "movement" here in our country. Let's not take this freedom for granted, dear one, for sometimes even I forget to do so. It truly is a precious gift.

Chapter 13

Meisje (I), walk the beach early in the morning, the sea breeze caressing my face. I hear the thundering wave upon wave crashing and crescendoing, soothing my soul, as the sun gently kisses me. Oh dear one, how blessed I feel to be alive, loved, healthy, and be one with everything around me! As I enjoy my surroundings, breathing in the fresh air, I cannot help but be thankful for being free. My cup is full to the brim overflowing with gratitude!

As I reflect back on my life's journey, I marvel at how God always seem to bring certain people into my life to help in my healing to wholeness. One particular person, an author and speaker, Corrie ten Boom, who was also a concentration camp survivor like me. She survived incarceration in several infamous concentration camps in Germany and lost all her family during the Holocaust.

From her I learned how to forgive. She was a wonderful friend and such a sweet child of God. She was very bold in sharing her story and her love for her savior Jesus Christ. She had courageousness in sharing the gospel, the good news, with whomever she met. She shared her story and the hardships she endured and how with God's help her bitterness had turned to "victory" through forgiveness!

I remember her telling me what a difficult time she had forgiving a certain prison guard who had been extra harsh and cruel to her sister Betsy. Many years later after WWII had ended, Corrie became a well-known author and speaker. In fact, the movie *The Hiding Place* was made about her life.

One day, Corrie was invited to speak at a church in Germany on the topic of forgiveness and on God's love and mercy. The cruel guard from the concentration camp, now a Christian, approached Corrie after the meeting with a smile on his face, beaming from ear to ear with an outstretched hand, he extended toward Corrie. Clearly, he expected her to be able to embrace and forgive him for what he had done since he too had become a believer. Well, Corrie just stood there, stiff and straight, with her arms down to her sides staring at this despised guard.

As she was transported back to that deplorable time and place in Ravensbruck concentration camp in Germany. She was frozen, trying desperately, praying hard, pleading with her Lord to give her strength, the love to forgive. She knew she needed to accept and shake the extended hand but she could not, she just couldn't, no matter how hard she tried to will, to force herself to do it. She just stood there for what seemed a very long time.

As I hear her telling me the story, I feel emotions so deep within myself as tears well up in my eyes. Just thinking about it stirs up memories, flashbacks, and dare I say, emotions of "hate" that I have carried in my own heart? Oh, dear one, Corrie and I are like one now. In tears, sobbing hard as I'm finding myself, trying, praying, pleading too! For God to give ME the strength and the love to forgive my captors of so long ago. Then I hear Corrie say, "I could not do it, Meisje, but He did. My precious Jesus did it for me!"

Then with tears streaming down my face, I fall into Corrie's arms. Embraced, enveloped as I feel with her His love, His forgiveness pouring over us, cleansing us with such an amazing grace and mercy. Lifting our arms, extending our hands, holding it toward our enemies realizing that they too are God's creation, even this particular guard. Now a fellow believer and a child of God the Father. Redeemed, forgiven, and saved, as Corrie and I are.

Dear one, when Corrie shared this story with me, all I felt was God's amazing love, mercy, and grace flooding me as I sobbed uncontrollably. I came away from this experience knowing that in order for me to forgive, I needed to know this overwhelming love, God's infinite love for me and all his children. For without this truth it's impossible to forgive. At least for me. I needed to be aware, to know that His love is directed to the person and for the person, for God hates the deed, the action, the sin, the perpetration, but he loves the person.

What a precious gift Corrie was to me! She came to California in her later years. I met her at our church where she came to speak and often came to visit as well. She lived not far from my home which made friendship easier to blossom and grow as well as having a commonality in being fellow survivors. It was nice we lived close to each other as I could stop by for a cup of tea. Of course, we would converse in our native tongue, Dutch, as she shared and told many stories.

During the war, her family hid a lot of Jews at the risk of their own lives and were involved in the Resistance. They had to be very careful, not daring to trust anyone as one never knew who would turn traitor which was precisely what happened. She and her family were turned in by someone who knew them and knew what they were doing. Hence, they were caught and imprisoned in a concentration camp.

Right after the war, Corrie became an ardent tramp for the Lord and tramped all over the world wherever God told her to go. She wrote her autobiography called *Tramp for the Lord: The Unforgettable True Story of Faith and Survival*. People, as well as I, got to know her through her books, as a speaker, and later through a movie adapted from her bestseller book *The Hiding Place*.

Let me share the poem I wrote about her, which I titled "Corrie ten Boom/Friend/Mentor."

Corrie ten Boom/Friend/Mentor

Corrie ... Bold ... Beautiful ... Loving ... Caring
Author ... Speaker ... Believer ... Follower of Christ.
God orchestrating a symphony the moment we met ...
Brilliant wonderful notes of music ... soothing ... comforting ...
A balm /ointment for a wounded soul ... mine ... just "Born again"

Truly a God thing our ... introduction ... meeting ... after you spoke.
An instant recognition ... kinship ... sisters in Christ ... I brand new ...
You a lifelong follower ... survivors, of concentration camps ... under
Germans ... Japanese ... Dutch language in common ... one healed ...
One wounded ... on road to recovery ... both "King's daughters"

Meisje ... Eurasian ... Touched ... Saved ... Redeemed
Artist ... Writer ... Believer ... Cleansed by her Savior.
God weaving ... the moment we shook hands ... a tapestry with ...
Brilliant colors ... smooth ... silken threads ... intertwined with existing
Dark dull colors ... a work in progress, the old gone, now a "New creation"

Truly a God thing using your pain ... hurt ... brokenness ... victorious life.
To mend ... lift ... draw ... form ... cement a relationship, through Christ
Receiving forgiveness ... undergoing healing, learning the power to love,
Japanese ... soldiers ... guards ... foe ... enemies ... those who've hurt, harmed.
Wounded ... now transformed ... soiled garments ... now "White as snow!"

For if you forgive men when they sin against you,
your heavenly Father will also forgive you!
—Matthew 6:14

Dedicated to Corrie ten Boom, God's "gift" to me!

It's so wonderful how God brought Corrie into my life and the timing of it as well. For I was a baby Christian compared to her. That is why I appreciated her wisdom and counsel on forgiveness. She had a very special relationship with her Jesus whom I had met in Jerusalem.

When I became a believer, I was thirsty for knowledge. Wanting to know more about God's Son, I delved into God's Word, signing up for Bible studies and joining different groups to further my knowledge. It was such an eye-opener to learn the history, theology, the Judeo/Christian beginnings, how the New Testament came into being, and how it intertwines with the Jewish roots in the Old Testament.

I just could not get enough studies under my belt, always wanting more and more to quench my thirst. But it was not until I went to the holy land with hubby and a group of people, and our pastor from our church that I got to meet God's Son for who He truly was and is! Wow, what an eye-opener that was! Seeing and experiencing things from the Bible, walking where He had walked, visiting places and surrounding areas where He lived, loved, and worked—the temple mount and synagogue where He taught. It was all very interesting, educational, emotional, and above all spiritual as the Bible and His Word came alive to me.

We even stayed in a Kibbutz for a couple of nights. We went to neighboring countries like Jordan to visit the Rose city, Petra, definitely a must see. We visited the pyramids in Egypt and the Cairo museum, and explored Turkey as well. To round off the biblical studies, the last five days was a cruise visiting the Greek islands, to visit all the places where Paul the apostle taught.

We even went to the island of Patmos where John wrote Revelation, the last book of the Bible in the New Testament. What an incredibly rich historical trip and study this was, steeped in antiquities as one encounters all the ancient cities, ruins, architecture, and archaeological sites as well as the people, their cultures, and their languages. In the holy land Israel, I was confronted with the humanity and Jewishness of God's Son, YESHUA (Hebrew)! My very first poem that I ever wrote was conceived and birthed from this educational biblical trip I took and I like to share it with you, dear one. I titled it "The Dawning."

The Dawning

Israel, Israel
  on the Kibbutz
Watching the early morning rays
  in the Rose garden
Flowers, flowers everywhere
  glistening in the sun
Still wet with drops of dew
  My Lord, my Savior
    Born a Jew

Poppies, Poppies
  on Mount Olive
Shining brightly inbetween the trees

in the Olive grove
Sorrow, pain, and agony
  of so long ago
Drinking the bitter cup ... suddenly I knew
  My Lord, my Savior
  A despised Jew

Jerusalem, Jerusalem
  on the hill
Walking through the hustle and bustle
  in the heart of the city
Taking in all the old and the new
  mingling with its people
Talking, listening, looking ... in awe
  My Lord, my Savior
  The Messiah.

Had I not been "born again" and living with a personal relationship with Christ when I met Corrie, our meeting would have been just that of someone coming to hear a fellow Dutch person speak about what she had gone through during WWII and incarceration in a concentration camp, just like I had gone through somewhat the same ordeal except mine was in the Pacific theater, hers in the European theater.

But that was not God's plan for both of us. Corrie was in her eighties (I, in my forties) when she was done "tramping" for the Lord and came to California to live out her later years practically next door to me, a mere ten to fifteen-minute ride by car. I clearly see God's hand in having orchestrated our meeting as I was very new in my faith and she was a lifelong believer. Corrie, almost at the end of her journey and mine the beginning.

Indeed, God has a plan and purpose for our lives and His plans are for good and not evil, to give us a future and a hope! (Jeremiah 29:11) Clearly, He preserved both of our lives, for her to be my friend and mentor.

In my case, God preserved my life for "such a time as this" (Esther 4:14); the 9/11 attack, my increased nightmares, the birthing of my poems, my speaking engagements, and my story, my book MEISJE!

Chapter 14

Battling survivor's guilt and forgiveness! How does one overcome? In my case, it's a process of digging deep into God's Word—reading, learning, and applying His teachings on that very subject. Letting go and letting God carry it for me seemed to work not very well for I found myself often still laden with unforgiveness and survivor's guilt. Yeshua, God's Son, reminds me He's the healer and restorer of brokenness. We are to come to Him when we are burdened down and heavy laden for His yoke is light. All beautiful wise words I understand the meaning of, I can visualize Him carrying it for me yet still, still, STILL I am laden!

His teachings are so opposite of what society says is right regarding guilt and forgiveness. He says if one slaps you on the cheek, turn your other cheek; if one has a need for a coat, give the one on your back. If one owes you a debt and can't pay it back, cancel it. He says do not hate your enemies but rather love your enemies! Wait, what, what, WHAT? Are there no consequences—don't we—don't they need to earn it? Work for it?

No! We are all imperfect people. We have all fallen short! In order to be perfect and whole and have peace, and a relationship with our heavenly Father, God had to send His Son. He had to come to rescue, to save, to ransom, to redeem. He came to pay the price with His blood, death, and resurrection. The perfect Lamb, God's only begotten Son became that perfect sacrifice, that sacrificial Lamb slain for our imperfections. Jewish laws require a blood SACRIFICE and God GIFTED us His Son! AMAZING GRACE!

You know what, dear ones? I finally got it. It took me awhile, no, actually a long time to understand that a gift indeed cannot be earned. You don't have to do anything for it either. Nor do you have to pay for it. There are no strings attached or conditions to be met, it is only to be accepted! Such amazing grace!

In regards to forgiveness, the key point is when you "forgive" it does not mean you "condone." We need to separate the deed from the person. When we can do that it frees us to condemn the action not the person. We are even allowed, even commanded to hate the sin which was perpetrated, but not the sinner who is the perpetrator. We need to read this many times over dear ones, until we get it! For God so loves the sinner, He gave us sinners the gift of forgiveness, by letting His only begotten Son pay the penalty which is death on the cross for our sins. A perfect wondrous, miraculous gift!

Dear one, I needed to learn these lessons, these truths, to see, to view those who have perpetrated and inflicted physical, emotional, and mental pain on me are God's children as well like you and me. Created and loved, albeit seriously flawed by their deeds and sins perpetrated. God LOVES the SINNER but HATES the SIN! And so must I, Meisje, do the same! In order to be forgiven, I need to forgive! And with God's help I, Meisje, did in order to be healed and made whole.

Although the wounds have healed and scabs have formed and covered it, it still can bleed when scratched or ripped open. Sometimes the pain and wounds can again be felt so deep and intense it overwhelms me! This usually happens right after a nightmare has occurred that brought me back to the concentration camp where suppressed memories have surfaced. This is what God wants me to deal with for my overall healing and wholeness. It has become easier for me to face my demons because I have learned to see the perpetrators as God's children and in need of forgiveness and God's love.

This brings me to Mama's horrific ordeal during our captivity which was witnessed by brother. It was a huge secret and sort of a mystery as well, remaining so even up until today. Plus a memory of an old crazy woman in the concentration camp both became recurring nightmares.

Let me share first about the old crazy woman before I share what happened to Mama. Here is the poem I wrote about the crazy old woman.

Crazy Old Woman

Piercing screams bolted me upright, heart racing
a mile a minute, clutching my chest, trying to orient
and see in the darkness, listening, as I shake uncontrollable!
Then I feel my husband's hand touch me and hear him say,
"It's okay, it's only a dream," as he soothes me back to sleep.

Suddenly I remember! Oh God, I remember this crazy old woman!
Every time we pass by her to get to our living quarters, the look on her
face, the wild eyes, the crazy things she did, scary things she said
and the most horrific piercing screams, mostly at night.

No Mama to comfort me, as I lay in this horrible place, a concentration camp
imprisoned, waiting for morning to rise and Mama to return!

So many questions about this crazy old woman stayed with me,
tucked deep down in my heart. Wondering what kind of punishment
would warrant and cause her to plunge into this darkness, this insanity?
As I lay soothed in my husband's arms, sleep overtakes me as I try
not to recall and remember WHAT and WHY this happened to her!

Then bits and pieces surface to my conscience, grappling with the
TRUTH as I lay there, trying to process, analyze as much as a five and a
half-year-old can; not succeeding, as darkness envelopes my heart
and mind. "Oh now I remember, I remember!" The crazy old woman
was punished, she was waterboarded because she refused to do what
was demanded! I finally fall asleep with arms around me, not Mama's, but God's!

I woke up close to 5 am and now sit at my computer,
as I hear my heavy breathing and feel myself shaking,
memories flooding back of this crazy old woman's screams and strange behavior.
I will myself to calm down, to stop shaking as I ask my heavenly Father to
be with me, help me bring to the surface the truth about what had
made this old woman in the concentration camp crazy!

Then fragmented pieces appear as I see her in my mind's eye. Shock and disbelief seeps into my consciousness. I burst out in uncontrollable sobs, shaking, and crying hard, calling God's name over and over, not believing the truth, sitting behind the computer, seeing myself as a child trying to process what I've heard and seen is truly the shocking TRUTH.

Oh dear God the Crazy "Old" Woman is not old, but a YOUNG *woman in her late teens or early twenties. Her dark hair turned gray overnight and her face aged considerably. Oh dear God I remember! She was young and beautiful like Mama! What happened? Oh, dear God she refused to* DO *the nightly* SEX ... SEX ... SEX *demanded of her. So, they* PUNISHED *her!* TORTURED *her!* WATERBOARDED *her!* DRIP, DRIP, DRIP! ENDLESSLY!

PROCESSING TRUTH!
Minutes later heaviness and darkness lifts. Stillness, calmness, dare I say peace, descends. A comfort surrounds me as I mourn the loss of innocence— the Crazy Old Woman's and my Mama's! As the morning light streams in, so does a light of dawning seep into my awareness, another truth my molestation of so long ago! Praise God for His Mercy, Grace, and HIS INFINITE LOVE!

Can you imagine, dear one, the shock I sustained from this awareness? The truth about this "old" woman being once a young vibrant woman, turning gray-haired and old overnight. I was not only shocked but traumatized again by the truth. Thank God I have my faith to draw strength from and to sustain me during the days ahead as I process the truth now as an adult and mourn the loss of our innocence.

The waterboarding this woman received left no physical scars, but the invisible wounds were sustained to her mind. They had restrained and bound her in such a way that she could only turn her head sideways but could not entirely avoid the systematic *drip, drip, drip* to her forehead. I imagine how it would feel not being able to turn off the constant *drip, drip, drip*. She probably knew exactly by counting between each drip, when the next drip would come and hit her forehead.

The only difference would be the placement on her face as she could only turn her head, not the rest of her body due to the ropes that bound and held her in place. My God, anyone would go insane! I already go nuts hearing the *drip, drip, drip* of a faucet let alone what this young woman underwent.

Poor, poor woman! I don't even know nor remember her name or what became of her. Other than that, I recall Mama telling me that one day she was taken away to an asylum for insane people. I cannot really tell you how long it took for the trauma of this realization to dissipate and the pain, a deep ache, ceased and finally stopped hurting.

As I'm writing this, I feel a tightness in my chest. It used to worry me but not anymore. Because now I know that after I stop and take a break from writing, especially if the recollection was a painful one, I come away with these type of chest pains which feels like an impending heart attack. No wonder nobody wants to talk about their experiences during the war or anything that they've endured. Believe me it hurts, it's painful! But I know there is nothing wrong with my heart other than that my wounds, the scabs—if scratched, can open and start bleeding again as I recount and share all this with you, dear one.

Now as promised, I want to share Mama's secret. However painful the recollection may be. Bear with me, dear one, please!

Mama's secret was so horrific that truly Meisje (I), cannot recall if I was a witness to it. But brother, during an interview with a Dutch representative for a possible eligible compensation at retirement age, finally told. Breaking down, sobbing uncontrollably, he confessed to witnessing Mama being gang raped by Japanese soldiers. I don't recall even seeing the consequences, the results of which was a pregnancy. Other than seeing Mama upon our liberation with an eighteen-month-old addition to our family.

I accepted the baby into the family and we endured hardships together, another incarceration, this time under the Indonesians for about six months. We never talked or asked questions about the sweet addition nor did I ever hear our parents talk about it. It remained a secret for a long time; as a matter of fact, it was years later in Holland when Mama told me about the circumstances of her pregnancy during the war which she asked me to keep it a secret.

Years later when Meisje was a married woman with children of her own, Mama asked again to keep it a secret. Meisje did promise her Mama she would as Mama was on her deathbed, but Meisje asked for one condition. The condition was if Meisje were to be asked the question if she knew the who, what, why, where of the pregnancy, she would not lie but tell what Mama had told her in secret. That's why even though our precious addition to our family wanted to know the truth of the circumstances to the pregnancy and her birth, Meisje could not give a satisfactory answer.

There was a conflicting report as to brother's account of witnessing Mama's rape by the Japanese guards versus the story told by Mama to Meisje, that the father was Indonesian and not a despised Japanese captor. Can you imagine, dear one, how and why all this still stays a secretive mystery? Of course, now it can be solved easily with DNA testing. But our dear precious addition is scared to choose that route and it is not mine to make. As I said before, how sad Mama and Papa never received or asked for counseling for dealing with these traumatic and horrific hardships and tortures endured during captivity in the concentration camps in Japan and the Dutch East Indies.

Chapter 15

Dear one, I too, carried a secret for a long, long time. But since God has placed it upon my heart that now, for such a time as this, that I share my story, I must share it all. It is painful to think, to remember the circumstances of my molestation. I want to express that there is healing of those physical, mental, and spiritual injuries, the moral injury that was done to me and others who are molested. It is through the gift of forgiveness. From God to me, and from me to my perpetrator. This poem is for those who have been molested, those who have healed, and those who are still struggling with the pain and trauma.

Molestation

Dark, darker, darkest ... night time, sleeping.
Shadow, enter, entering, entered ... family member.
Awakening, awakened, awake ... aware!
Touch, touching, touched ... kiss, kissing, kissed.
Sleep, sleeping, slept ... breathe, breathing, breath.
Pretend, pretending, pretended ... happen,
Happening, happened ... surprised.
Shiver, shivering ... sweat, sweating ... feel ... feeling helpless.
Thrust, thrusting ... push ... pushing ... pushed.
Hard, harder ... stiff, stiffer ... poke, poking ... poked.
Cry, crying, cries ... moan, moaning, moans.
Hurt, hurting ... ache, aching ... pain, pains!
Big, bigger, biggest ... Huge!
Plunge ... plunging ... plunged ... semen!

Dark, darker, darkest ... feverish ... NIGHTMARE.
Fall, falling ... deep, deeper, deepest hole ... Pit.
Cold, colder ... numb ... numbness ... Paralyze,
paralyzing, paralyzed. Physically ... Mentally.
Die, dying ... slow, slowly ... breath by ... breath
Lay, laying ... curl, curling ... fetus position,
wait, waiting ... want, wanting ... DEATH!
Awakened, awakening ... awoke to a Light.
Enter, entering ... entered ... person, a Presence!
Light, lighter ... bright, brighter ... brightest Light!
Shine, shining ... blind, blinding ... warm ... warmer.
Descends, descending ... deep, deeper ... down the PIT.
Touch, touching, touched ... embrace, embracing, embraced.
Envelope, enveloping, enveloped, by LIGHT ... PRESENCE!
Carry, carrying, carried ... lift, lifting, lifted.
Up, up ... upwards ... out, out ... mire, slimy pit ... kiss, kissing.
Drip, dripping ... spill, spilling ... drop, drops ... lots!
Lick, licking ... taste, tasting ... Blood! His, God's, Yeshua's
Bleeding, bled ... dying, dead ... rising, risen ... rose!
Redeem, redeeming ... rescue, rescuing ... salvaging
Meisje, a wretch, me ... lovingly, mercifully, graciously!

Chapter 16

Thank God for new beginnings, for new chapters, new seasons, new phases in one's life, don't you agree, dear one? A fresh start! That's how I dealt with my molestation perpetrated by a family member. Through counseling, help from the church, support groups, loving family, and friends, I overcame successfully the pain, the darkness, the ugliness of it by forgiving! By having learned to separate the "deed" what was done to me by the "perpetrator" and for learning that it is okay to "hate" the "deed," meaning one does not have to "condone" the action that was perpetrated.

That is why I could separate the "sin" (deed) from the "sinner" (person) because that's how my heavenly Father deals with it. He teaches to always hate the sin but commands us to love the sinner. I admit it is not always easy; easier said than done indeed! But very important for my overall recovery, well-being and wholeness.

During our captivity, I came to not only accept the precious addition of my new baby sister but formed a very special bond and relationship with her that I've treasured throughout the years. This precious addition became my very special Sissy. Over the years especially as an adult, I've come not to only love and cherish her but to admire her tremendously for having overcome such dire, turbulent, and secretive beginnings.

Sissy did not have an easy life growing up, she endured hardships as an adult and struggled to overcome doing it in her own way as best she could. Always knowing instinctively, she was and felt different from her siblings. Even though no one told her and this was kept a family secret for years and years until she was sixty years old. My fervent prayer and hope is that one day Sissy can forgive, move on, and allow herself to rise above it. For Sissy deserves the very best

God has to offer her which is His amazing grace. This is the poem I wrote and gifted Sissy on her birthday that expresses my special feelings and fondness for her!

Sister (Sissy)

What a beautiful thing
Your life and mine
intertwined for sixty years.
A tapestry in God's design
woven in most areas
with vibrant-colored threads.
But in some places
embroidered in are
dark-and-dull colors.
A canvas in the making
this wondrous design
shrouded in mystery
'n conceived in secrecy.
God formed and made you
in utter seclusion in
our Mother's womb
For a special plan
and purpose.
Your miraculous birth
In the midst of hardship
and trials in the concentration
camp and our survival
Were the very first threads
woven in the fabric
of God's design.
We will trust and believe
the finished piece will
one day be exactly according
to His plan and blueprint.

For only then
are we able to view
the upper side
And know why pain,
Tears, and sickness
were intertwined in the
tapestry of our life.
And it is now with deep
Gratitude and thanksgiving
That I wish you a
beautiful birthday
A wonderful evening
and an awesome year,
With God's special blessings!

As I said before, my fervent prayer and hope is for Sissy to overcome, and also to come to know God's amazing grace in Messiah Yeshua, our Lord.

But I will restore you to health and heal your wounds," declares the Lord.
—Jeremiah 30:16

For I know the plans I have for you, says the Lord. They are plans for good and not for evil, to give you a hope and a future.
—Jeremiah 29:11

Meisje's love and admiration for her Mama is equally strong as that she has toward Sissy. Just the thought that Mama could have opted to abort but did not. What a choice to consciously have chosen to carry and keep this precious addition. I often have wracked my brains trying to think back how Mama managed to keep Sissy sheltered, alive, and cared for in addition to us her other children.

It might very well be that one day that recollection will surface, but the knowledge of Sissy's existence for me began when we were liberated, that is when I was first aware of having her in our midst during our imprisonment in the horrific Bersiap civil war. Putting myself in Mama's shoes as a mother myself now, it's difficult to consider if I could have made that same decision to keep instead of aborting. Even though like Mama, I've gone through and survived the atrocities during our captivity, I don't think I could have made the same choice as she did. A hard choice indeed for Mama and very brave. This shows a deep unconditional love for what was growing and becoming an integral part of her. Unbelievable and incredible too that Sissy made it through. She survived and did not succumb to death like so many other babies and young children. A miracle thanks to Mama. Here is a poem dedicated to my courageous Mama.

Mama

I remember her as it were yesterday
'cause I carry her in my heart.
A petite graceful slender woman
with straight long dark hair
and a sunny disposition.
Who loved music and the arts
had a heart for the downtrodden
wayward kids and stray animals.
Our house was always filled with lots
of music, songs, books, and kids.
She was good at loving and hugging,
mentoring, caring, and encouraging
especially young and upcoming artists.
A beautiful singer, an avid reader,
wonderful hostess with a flair for
making everybody feel welcome.
I remember her mostly as "Sunny"
a nickname of her choosing.
A wonderful name to remind herself

she is a survivor, overcoming the
darkness and ugliness, she'd endured.
Victorious most of the time
battling, struggling, combatting
illnesses, and deep depressions.
Our Mama such an inspiration,
a role model of strength in weakness.
Leaving us a wonderful legacy, in
that life is about choices we make.
To always see the lighter side of things
a cup half full instead of empty and that
there is sunshine after every rain storm.

I'm so thankful Mama decided to keep and not abort Sissy and for her immensely unconditional love for this special child, despite the circumstances, cost to her own life, and the hardship it must have been. I applaud, admire, and love you for your braveness, Mama! And you, my special Sissy, who I adore for your courage in facing life—living, learning, laughing, loving!

Chapter 17

Meisje (I), love walking in the early mornings and do so every day. Though I vary my route, it consists of tramping the hills in my neighborhood and then going down to walk the beach. The fresh ocean air and sea breeze, the sound of thundering waves, crashing, foaming, always forming surprisingly different swirls and patterns, this soothes my soul, refreshes my spirit, overflows me with gratitude, and thanksgiving. Plus, it's quite a nice workout, much better than in the gym. It's free, no membership fees either. Of course, walking is a good workout especially in a hilly neighborhood. I recommend it highly, it's an excellent healthy exercise.

Often after her walk and having showered, Meisje likes to sit on her deck that overlooks the ocean or in the courtyard which has several cozy sitting areas. Today she opens the French doors to her courtyard to sit with a cup of coffee and to have a leisurely breakfast. She brought a book to read as well as her journal while listening to the music wafting from the family room behind her through the open French doors. Enjoying her breakfast consisting of a waffle, scrambled eggs, and a bowl of fruits, savoring every bite, every morsel. Feeling so blessed and lucky, sitting in a comfortable wicker chair, soaking up the morning sunshine as the music soothingly caresses her.

As she listened to an Andrea Bocelli tape, her favorite piece came on—the strains of *Time To Say Goodbye;* enveloped and captured her heart and soul as never before.

Then without warning, tears came streaming down her face. As she listened to this beautiful and moving song, she was transported back to the concentration camp. Remembering, seeing scenes in her mind's eye as she was transported back in time to captivity, she remembers hearing beautiful sounds coming from somewhere other than Meisje's quarters. Sounds of music so beautifully stirring, heavenly; as Mama, I, and others started to move toward where it came from. As we came closer to the source of music, a crowd already had gathered and we inched closer to listen. We could not see if it was a radio or a phonograph. But drawn like moths to a candle light, we stood transfixed to hear the most beautiful music, sounds so hauntingly yet so heavenly.

Gripping us, soothing, caressing, breathlessly capturing us, we dared not move or make a sound. Hoping and praying we wouldn't get caught as we let the music lift us out from this "Hellish" pit and transport us briefly to a "Heavenly" place!

As I sit in the courtyard with tears streaming down my face to the ending of *Time to Say Goodbye*, I cannot believe we were able to witness such a miraculous event such a long time ago in the concentration camp. Of course, reflecting and looking back I remember now that incident was not without consequences. For I remember asking Mama years later, and her telling me, that it happened close to the time of liberation and the person was caught and punished.

Rumors circulated that additional people were punished as well. Some prisoners were put in sweat boxes. The same as the person who was caught. To be placed in a sweat box is a horrible form of punishment. It truly is a form of the worst torture. It is a wooden box, only large enough for one person to remain in a standing position. The prisoner is kept in this box for hours, sometimes even days. Sitting or squatting is impossible, though some do, collapsing into a twisted, contorted mess.

The prisoner always ended up losing consciousness due to heat exhaustion and dehydration. I don't know how many died or ended up in the hospital. I do remember hearing about and reading about this type of torture which often ended in death.

Other prisoners were punished by doubling up tasks or assigning extra jobs. Usually that called for the most despised job of carrying heavy barrels with overflowing human waste to a dump site located quite a distance away from the camp. And of course, if you've been paired with someone shorter or taller than yourself, it caused spillage. For it takes two people to manage and shoulder the bamboo poles carrying the barrelful of human feces and urine. Such a horrible, humiliating, and demeaning job for any person. Because prisoners already felt worthless, weak, sick, and stripped of any dignity, they put up with these tasks and duties whether assigned, punished, or meted out.

Why all of a sudden this beautiful duet sung by Andrea Bocelli and Sarah Brightman evoked these memories surprises me since I've heard the song many times before. But I'm glad it did stir up suppressed memories so I can deal and face my demons once again. Thank God it happened in my own home, in familiar surroundings, in this peaceful setting, in my beautiful courtyard. Yet what I just experienced, the feelings, emotions, and deep sense of stirrings in the depth of my soul was something indescribably beautiful. Almost as beautiful as that first experience so long ago imprisoned in the concentration camp, now reliving those beautiful sweet strains of music once again.

No wonder I love and appreciate classical music. Now I realize even more so why classical music occupies such a special place in my heart. For I now see so clearly how my heavenly Father has orchestrated my life into this beautiful symphony, woven it from my birth throughout captivity, to my cozy, sweet Holland; to big, bold, beautiful America. This journey of mine ...

> God had planned it and purposed it, for such a
> time as this!
> —Jeremiah 29:11 and Esther 4:14

In closing, let me share with you, this last poem of mine which I think is the perfect one to end with.

Symphony

Staggering and beautiful...recalling details that eluded her before
Due to initial fears... sharply etched deep within her soul...
Emerged from the seas of wounds that had covered them,
Remembering millions minute details. Important incidents,
Horrid nights, tender moments, atrocities, abandonments...
Horrific days, tortured screams, days, nights,
Agonizing waves of hunger, body ravaged by Malaria, Beriberi,
Dysentery, Scurvy, Head lice and open Sores.
Tormented, weakened physically, mentally,
Remembering being carried by
Wave upon wave of the most beautiful sweet strains
of a heavenly Symphony!
Women, children crowded close to the source where the music was
coming from.
Swept up in the middle of the day; drawn, pulled, lifted up
To the most thrilling sounds.
Whispers, shivers, excitements as stillness, quietness descended,
Careful, for guards!
Transfixed, heaven bound, crying, weeping, wounded bodies,
Minds, souls, as they were enveloped, enfolded embraced by
This most wondrous stirring classical symphony!
Beautifully indwelled by the music, truly a balm,
an ointment to the crushed spirit
Souls sponging, soaking, drinking in the lyrics,
notes, melodies,
Angelic voices and Instruments...
Strings, harps, violins, piano, organ
Showering, drenching all, with a glimmer of
HOPE, FAITH & JOY!

Now years later, looking back she could see why God orchestrated,
Allowed her "Life" to flow and crash like waves upon thundering waves,
Crescendoing at times so peacefully, serenely, soothingly and calmly,
Cresting, riding, resting, embraced, enveloped In God's mercies, grace,
Healing touch, protection, provision, peace and infinite love!
No longer, really questioning the "WHY" of it all but accepting
The purpose and plan He had laid out so beautifully for her!
Forced moves from two countries to
America where upon entering the harbor in New York,
A Lady beckoned her,
Welcomed her with open arms to live the "LIFE"
GOD Designed, Orchestrated and Purposed
for such a time as this!
— Jeremiah 29:11 and Esther 4:14

Dear one,

How strange to say goodbye to you, to not continue to share things anymore. I guess I became so comfortable in sharing even the very intimate minute things with you like I would with a "bestie," a best friend. Or maybe, I'm not ready to say goodbye yet. Yeah, that's probably it, so let's not! Maybe we should say, "Until next time!" What do you think? Maybe I will write another book and take you along with me again? Oh, that would be fun!

Anyway, dear one, I want to thank you for having come alongside with me on this journey of mine though this is not the end of it. I feel like I'm still on a path, a journey of God's choosing. But now I get to enjoy the symphony He has orchestrated. Isn't he wonderful, dear one? God's love is HUGE!

Well, dear ones, until we meet again I bid you farewell. Please know that you are much loved, appreciated, and cherished beyond measure!

God Bless!
Big hug and with much gratitude,
Meisje

PS, I leave you with God's word, Ephesians 3:14–20, a reminder of God's amazing love for each of you!

Ephesians 3:14–20

*When I think of the wisdom and
scope of God's plan, I fall to my knees
and pray to the Father, the Creator of
everything in heaven and earth. I
pray that from His glorious, unlimited
resources He will give you mighty
inner strength through His Holy Spirit.
And I pray that Christ will be more
and more at home in your hearts as
you trust in Him. May your roots go
down deep into the soil of God's
marvelous love. And may you have
the power to understand, as all God's
people should, how wide, how long,
how high, and how deep His love
really is. May you experience the love
of Christ, though it is so great you
will never fully understand it. Then
you will be filled with the fullness of
life and power that comes from God.
Now glory be to God! By His
mighty power at work within us, He is
able to accomplish infinitely more
than we would ever dare to ask, or hope.
May He be given glory in the church
and in Christ Jesus forever and
ever through endless ages. Amen!*

About the Author

Charlotte Van Steenbergen was born in Indonesia, then known as the Dutch East Indies. She and her mother and two siblings were forced into a concentration camp by the Japanese as prisoners of war during the Japanese occupation of the South Pacific during WWII. The especially cruel punishment by the Kempeitai was due to Charlotte's father not only serving in the military but also having been secretly recruited by the US intelligence. This was his secret to bear for up to twenty to twenty-five years after the war when he could finally beg his wife for forgiveness for the hell she endured.

After three years in this prison nicknamed Hell, Charlotte and her family were liberated by US and allied forces only to be imprisoned again due to their European heritage during the civil war between the Indonesians and the Dutch government. After escaping this prison, Charlotte and her family fled to the Netherlands and then were granted immigration to the United States via the Pastore Walter Immigration Act of 1956. Charlotte and her husband are proud US citizens and live happily in Southern California, where they enjoy time with their grown children and their spouses and their four grandchildren. The seeds that were planted in Hell produced over the years, brought Charlotte to the saving grace and a loving relationship with Jesus Christ.

CPSIA information can be obtained
at www.ICGtesting.com
Printed in the USA
FSHW012339130119
54979FS